THE
ABCs
OF SHAREPOINT

26 WAYS SHAREPOINT CAN ENHANCE YOUR DIGITAL WORKPLACE

by Nate Chamberlain

ISBN: 979-8-8609-7395-4

Independently published

TABLE OF CONTENTS

DEDICATION

This edition, like the first, is dedicated with enduring love to my grandma, **Judith "Gummy" McMillen**.

The joy of seeing her hold the first edition remains a cherished memory. Though she isn't here to witness the second edition, her influence is deeply interwoven throughout its pages and served as a driving force behind its completion. Gummy was a beacon of strength, grace, and boundless love. Her infectious laughter and enduring lessons continue to guide and inspire us. Her spirit, though missed every day, remains ever-present in our hearts and stories.

INTRODUCTION

Five years have zipped by since The ABCs of SharePoint first popped up as the 100th blog post over at SharePointLibrarian.com (now NateChamberlain.com). Back then, I wanted to mark that milestone in a big way. Now, looking back, it's kind of wild to see how much SharePoint has changed and grown since the first edition of this book in 2018.

This second edition, updated in September of 2023, is for you if:

- You're just stepping into the world of SharePoint.
- You're already friends with SharePoint but want new ideas or just a fun alphabetic journey through various concepts.
- You thought the book's cover would look nice on your shelf

Inside, you'll find answers to:

- What's SharePoint these days?
- What awesome things can we do with it?

Just like the original, I've gone from A-Z, trying to pick out a fun SharePoint feature for every letter of the alphabet.

Now, for my friends with SOS (Shiny Object Syndrome) like me:

Reading about all this neat stuff might get you super excited. But remember, just because you can do something, doesn't mean you should jump right in. Test things out somewhere safe before you tinker with your main setup. And hey, chat with your team – let them know what you're thinking of trying out so everyone's on the same page.

Alright, ready? Buckle up, slide on those sunglasses, and let's dive back into the shiny cityscape of SharePoint!

ABOUT NATE CHAMBERLAIN

Nate Chamberlain is a firm believer in the transformative power of Microsoft 365, both in its practical application and its broader community. Residing in Kansas City, Missouri, with his husband William and their feline companions, Baxter and Lia,  Nate finds joy in merging his personal and professional experiences, always prioritizing growth and understanding.

Having been honored as a 5x Microsoft MVP, Nate also holds certifications like the M365 Enterprise Administrator Expert, Microsoft Power Platform App Maker Associate, Microsoft Teams Administrator Associate, and CompTIA CTT+. But these aren't just badges; they symbolize the time, dedication, and real-world experiences that have shaped his expertise in the realm of Microsoft 365.

Nate's eagerness to share knowledge is evident not just in his work but in his outreach efforts. His YouTube channel has caught the attention of over a million viewers, and his blog at NateChamberlain.com has served as a resource for more than 2 million visitors. As the author of several books on M365 topics, he's continuously driven by a desire to assist others in navigating the Microsoft 365 landscape.

Beyond the digital world, Nate's zest for sharing stories finds another outlet at the Kansas City Zoo, where he serves as a volunteer docent, talking about the fascinating world of wildlife and conservation with guests.

In all his endeavors, whether they be tech-oriented, through online platforms, or at the zoo, Nate's goal is the same: to inform, connect, and inspire. He remains a strong advocate for the value of community engagement, shared knowledge, and collaborative growth.

CONNECT WITH NATE:

- **Website**: NateChamberlain.com
- **YouTube**: youtube.com/NateChamberlain
- **LinkedIn**: linkedin.com/in/nchambe

WHAT, EXACTLY, IS SHAREPOINT?

Imagine the scene: You're at a family dinner, waxing poetic about using SharePoint at work. Your brother-in-law (or other family member), busy with a mound of mashed potatoes, interrupts with, "What's SharePoint? Is that like PowerPoint?"

The easy route? Flash a grin, say yes, and ask for the gravy. But let's be a good SharePoint advocate in this scenario and attempt an explanation.

Rather than a static digital space or folder, envision SharePoint as a lively digital city where documents, pages, and news harmoniously interact with their creators, modifiers, and readers. Positioned at the heart of Microsoft 365, SharePoint enables users to:

- **Co-author documents:** Experience collective creation in real-time!
- **Manage versions seamlessly:** End the "versionX.docx" nightmare.
- **Design and distribute forms:** Think of them as efficient digital memos.
- **Automate mundane tasks:** Embrace smart automation. No more monotony!
- **Enhance data security:** A robust shield for your files.

- **Engage and socialize:** Emulate water cooler chats, minus the cooler.
- **Customize your workspace:** A digital hub tailored for your team.
- **Upgrade collaboration:** Swap physical whiteboards for always-available-from-anywhere lists.
- **Organize communications:** Transform legacy "reply all" email threads into comment threads or conversations.
- **Personalize alerts:** Curate your news and manage your focus.
- **Merge information:** Integrate data without repetition.

Hankering for the shorter, gravy-passing pitch?

> *"SharePoint Online is where teams craft, collaborate, and curate, making the digital grind delightfully interactive."*

Even shorter?

> *"SharePoint is our online hub for collaboration."*

They said Microsoft Teams is cooler?

> *"Actually, SharePoint is the backbone of Microsoft Teams."*

They said Slack is cooler?

> *"I'm sorry, something's just come up and we have to leave dinner early."*

Honed in on your SharePoint elevator speech now? Excellent! Now, back to those mashed potatoes.

A | ACCESSIBILITY

In the diverse landscape of the modern digital workplace, ensuring that SharePoint Online is accessible to all users is paramount. Just as a city strives to accommodate everyone, SharePoint is designed to be inclusive, allowing all users to effectively navigate and interact with its features. That's why the **A** of our ABCs is for **Accessibility**.

IMMERSIVE READER: INCLUSIVE CONTENT CONSUMPTION

In the pursuit of making SharePoint truly accessible to everyone, the Immersive Reader feature offers powerful functionality. It includes:

- **Immersive reading mode:** When viewing a SharePoint document in either the web or desktop versions of Word, select **View | Immersive Reader**. Immersive Reader is a built-in tool that promotes content consumption for users with varying reading abilities. It allows users to customize text appearance, such as font size and style, background color, and spacing, tailoring the reading experience to their needs.

Figure 1 - Settings panel when using Immersive Reader

- **Text-to-speech and language translation options:**
  Immersive Reader offers a text-to-speech feature that can read content aloud, making it accessible to those with reading difficulties or visual impairments. Multiple language support ensures that content can be understood by speakers of different languages, promoting global inclusivity.

- **Breakdown of complex words:** SharePoint's Immersive Reader breaks down complex words into syllables, making it easier for users with reading challenges to grasp the content.

- **Grammar and comprehension aids:** It provides grammar highlighting and parts-of-speech labels.

By incorporating the Immersive Reader feature into your SharePoint environment, you're not just accommodating individuals with various accessibility needs, but also enriching the digital landscape of collaboration and knowledge sharing, making it accessible, welcoming, and truly inclusive for all.

ENHANCING NAVIGATION FOR VISUAL ACCESSIBILITY

Navigating SharePoint with visual impairments is akin to using tactile pathways in a city to find your way. SharePoint offers features that enhance navigation and ensure content is perceivable:

Keyboard Navigation:

- Navigate through SharePoint using keyboard shortcuts for better control and accessibility.
- Use **Tab** and arrow keys to move between elements and interact with them.

Screen Reader Compatibility:

- SharePoint is compatible with screen readers like JAWS and NVDA, providing audio cues and descriptions of content.
- Use headings, lists, and alternative text to ensure content is properly conveyed.

DOCUMENT ACCESSIBILITY FOR ALL USERS

Just as a well-lit city street accommodates both pedestrians and cyclists, SharePoint ensures that documents are accessible to everyone, regardless of their abilities:

Accessible Document Formats:

- Create documents in formats like Word and PowerPoint with accessibility features such as headings, alt text for images, and descriptive links.
- Use built-in accessibility checkers to identify and fix potential issues.

Alternative Text for Images:

- Add alternative text to images to provide context for screen reader users.

- Describe images concisely and accurately for a meaningful understanding.

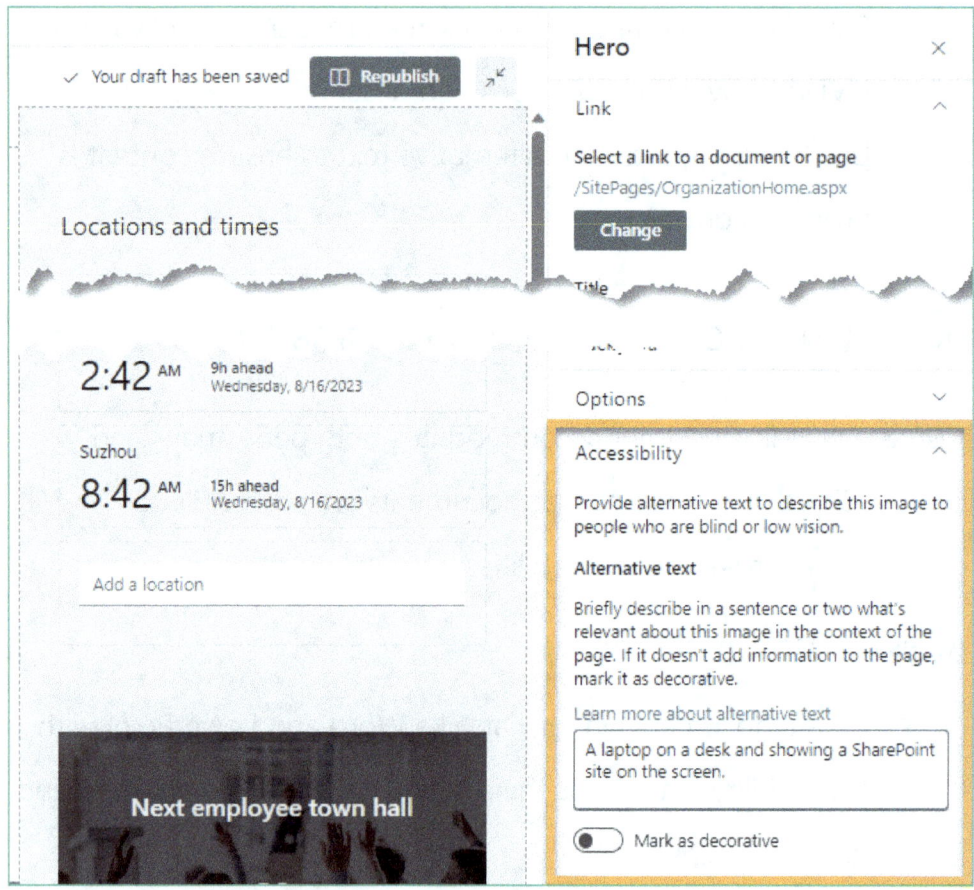

Figure 2 - Settings panel for an image showing the Accessibility section expanded

ENABLING COLLABORATION AND INTERACTION

Inclusive collaboration in SharePoint is like participating in a city-wide conversation. SharePoint's collaborative features ensure that users of all abilities can contribute effectively:

Screen Reader Support for Co-Authoring:

- Collaborate on documents with screen reader users in real time, ensuring everyone's input is valued.
- Receive audio cues about changes and contributions as you work together.

Accessible Comments and Feedback:

- Leave comments in documents that are perceivable by screen readers.
- Ensure that feedback and discussions are accessible to all team members.

By embracing accessibility features within SharePoint, you're fostering an environment where all users, regardless of their abilities, can participate fully and contribute meaningfully.

B | BUSINESS INTELLIGENCE AND DASHBOARDS

MAKING DATA WORK FOR YOU

In our SharePoint City, data is like the daily news – always changing and vital for decision-making. Let's explore how SharePoint uses dashboards and charts to turn numbers into clear, useful visuals. Welcome to letter **B**, **business intelligence and dashboards**.

DATA VISUALIZATION: DASHBOARDS AND WEB PARTS

Think of dashboards in SharePoint like a bulletin board prominently displayed along our city's main streets, showing key info for everyone to see as they traverse the digital routes of their daily work. There are two web parts that are exceptionally suited for this:

- **Power BI web part:** Imagine a city bulletin board that updates itself with the latest news from one or several sources. The

Power BI Web Part brings live, changing reports straight into SharePoint, making data come alive.

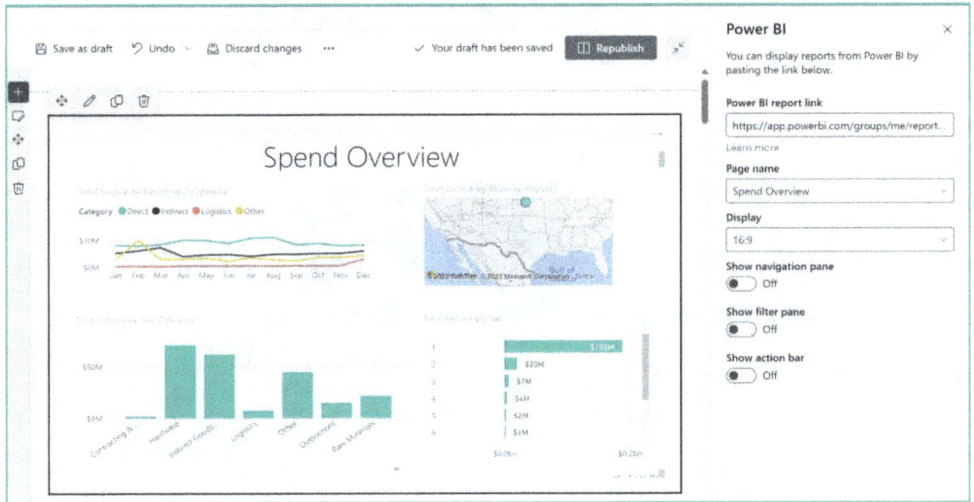

Figure 3 - Power BI web part being configured on a SharePoint page

- **Quick chart web part:** This is a straightforward tool for showing data. Picture a simple sign in the city square that changes as the weather does. The Quick chart web part turns SharePoint list or library data into charts that update by themselves as the source list or library is updated. It's easy to use, and you don't need Power BI or any other tools.

Figure 4 - Quick chart web part being configured on a SharePoint page

The big difference? Power BI has a sharper learning curve and requires that viewers are licensed to use Power BI. But it can incorporate multiple lists, workbooks, etc., even if they're from different sites, as data sources and become a one-stop shop for those seeking its insights. It can be one visual (chart) or it can be a report page with many different visuals and slicers sharing the web part's real estate.

The Quick chart web part, on the other hand, is intuitive and easy to set up, but is limited to manually entered data or a single list or library on your site. It can also only be represented as a single visual – either a column chart or a pie chart.

HOW DO YOU ADD A WEB PART?

1. As a site member or owner, select **Edit** in the upper right corner of the page or news post to which you want to add the web part.

2. Then select the plus (**+**) symbol when hovering in the section area in which you'd like to place the web part.

3. Search for and select either **Power BI** or **Quick chart**.

WHY USE POWER BI IN SHAREPOINT?

Adding Power BI to SharePoint takes your data game to the next level. Here's why it's a good move:

- **From Static to Dynamic:** While SharePoint lists and quick charts show a glimpse or fragment of a larger picture, Power BI shows the moving, changing story in its entirety and can be drilled up and down to the level appropriate for the viewer. It's the difference between a single photo or short film and a movie.

- **Zoom In or Out:** Just as you can look at different parts of a city map, with Power BI, you can focus on specific details or get a broad view of your data. Your executives likely want the entire cityscape at the helicopter level, whereas your HR managers likely want to focus on a specific zone within the organization.

- **Consolidate Data Across Lists/Sources:** Instead of scattered bits of data on various sites in multiple lists and files, bring everything together in one clear view. Less context switching, more informed decision-making.
- **Interactive Tools:** With Power BI, you don't just look at data; you can interact with it, ask questions, and find new insights.

BENEFITS OVER BASIC CHARTS AND LISTS

Power BI offers some real advantages:

- **Always up-to-date:** Unlike static charts that wait for updates or manual publishing, Power BI dashboards can be set to auto-refresh, always showing the latest info without the need for human intervention.
- **Dive deeper:** Go beyond just seeing data – understand it and the underlying relationships. Why did one number go up while another went down?
- **Share findings:** Talk about what you discover, share insights with your team, and make decisions together.
- **Combine data:** Mix and match data from different places, so you get the full picture in one place.

With business intelligence and dashboards in SharePoint, understanding data becomes simple and clear. In our journey through SharePoint City, tools like Power BI and the Quick chart web part help make sense of the numbers, turning them into clear, easy-to-understand visuals. As we keep exploring, we'll find more ways SharePoint can help make work easier and more effective.

C | COMPLIANCE AND GOVERNANCE

For letter **C**, let's delve into the pivotal world of **compliance and governance** within SharePoint. Just as a city requires regulations and structures to function effectively, SharePoint equips you with tools to ensure content integrity, adhere to regulations, and foster orderly collaboration.

ENSURING CONTENT INTEGRITY: YOUR DIGITAL FRAMEWORK

SharePoint enables you to establish a structured digital environment where content remains organized and secure. Here's a glimpse into maintaining content integrity:

- **Document libraries:** Think of these as designated zones. SharePoint's libraries provide a structured space for storing documents, ensuring consistency in naming, versioning, and access.

- **Metadata and taxonomy:** Imagine these as labeling systems. SharePoint allows you to tag content with relevant metadata and apply taxonomy, making it easier to locate and manage information.

NAVIGATING COMPLIANCE: STAYING ALIGNED AND SECURE

Just as adhering to city codes is essential, SharePoint helps you uphold regulatory compliance and security. Here's how it aids in maintaining compliance:

- **Retention policies:** Think of these as digital archiving. Retention policies in Microsoft 365 let you define how long content is retained, archived, or disposed of to meet legal and regulatory requirements.
- **Audit logs:** Imagine these as digital footprints. SharePoint tracks user activities, such as deletion of files, ensuring accountability and enabling you to respond to compliance inquiries and meet regulatory requirements.
- **Version control:** Think of this as content evolution. SharePoint's built-in version control maintains a history of changes for pages, news, documents, and list items, allowing you to revert to previous states if needed. In most cases, just

right-click a document or list item and select **Version History**
to access it. For pages and news, select **Page details** at the top
of the page to find version history.

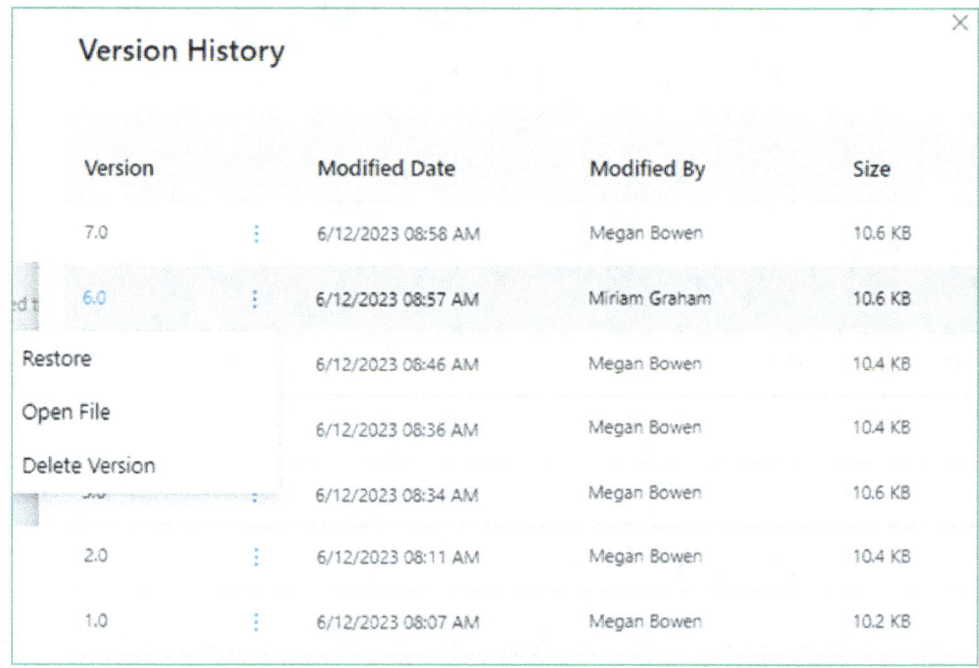

Figure 5 - Version history for a SharePoint file

GOVERNANCE: ORCHESTRATING THE DIGITAL ECOSYSTEM

Governance is like the city administration—it sets the rules and
policies that guide SharePoint's usage. Establishing effective
governance ensures a thriving digital ecosystem. Consider these
aspects:

- **User guidelines:** Just as a city has rules for residents, SharePoint governance outlines user expectations and best practices for content creation, sharing, and collaboration. This may also include material akin to a code of conduct.

- **Site hierarchies:** Think of these as planning zones. Governance defines how sites are structured into hubs, helping users find information efficiently and maintaining a coherent and consistent digital landscape.

- **Data lifecycle management:** Governance also oversees how content is created, used, and retired, ensuring efficient data management throughout its lifecycle. You may have retention schedules in place already for legacy files – that's a great starting place for configuring the SharePoint side of things.

By implementing SharePoint's compliance and governance features, you're essentially investing in a sturdy digital infrastructure. It safeguards content, aligns your organization with regulations, and enhances collaboration in a structured manner.

D | DOCUMENT COLLABORATION

In the sprawling digital metropolis of SharePoint, document collaboration emerges as a central square, bustling with ideas, conversation, and innovation. Just as cities thrive on shared spaces and mutual endeavors, SharePoint facilitates a symbiotic environment where documents are not merely stored but evolve through collective inputs. This brings us to letter **D, document collaboration**.

SEAMLESS COLLABORATION: THE HEART OF PRODUCTIVITY

At the core of SharePoint's document collaboration is a seamless synergy, reminiscent of communal spaces in a city where every individual contributes to the collective spirit. Dive into this collaborative heartbeat:

- **Real-time co-authoring:** This is like brainstorming in a city square. Multiple users can work on the same document simultaneously, making edits in real-time, sparking ideas off one another, and driving swift decisions. Each user sees where all other users are in the document when opened and editing simultaneously, and nobody has to be the sole transcriber anymore. Gone are the days of fifteen versions of a document with individual edits being sent to a poor soul tasked with consolidating all revisions.

- **Version history:** Look familiar? We talked about version history from a compliance and governance perspective. But it's also important from a day-to-day collaboration perspective. Version history chronicles your document's journey. Just as cities have historical landmarks, SharePoint chronicles every twist and turn of your document, offering the option to revisit and reinstate previous versions. This transparency promotes both accountability and bold exploration. Undo mistakes, compare progress, and witness collaborative evolution. The best part? Any site member can view and utilize version history – it's not restricted to owners or admins.

Like city plazas that catalyze community interactions, SharePoint is the launchpad that facilitates fluid content creation:

- **Document templates:** These are your foundational blueprints. You can add your own document templates to any library on your site, streamlining the document creation process for members while preserving consistency across content.

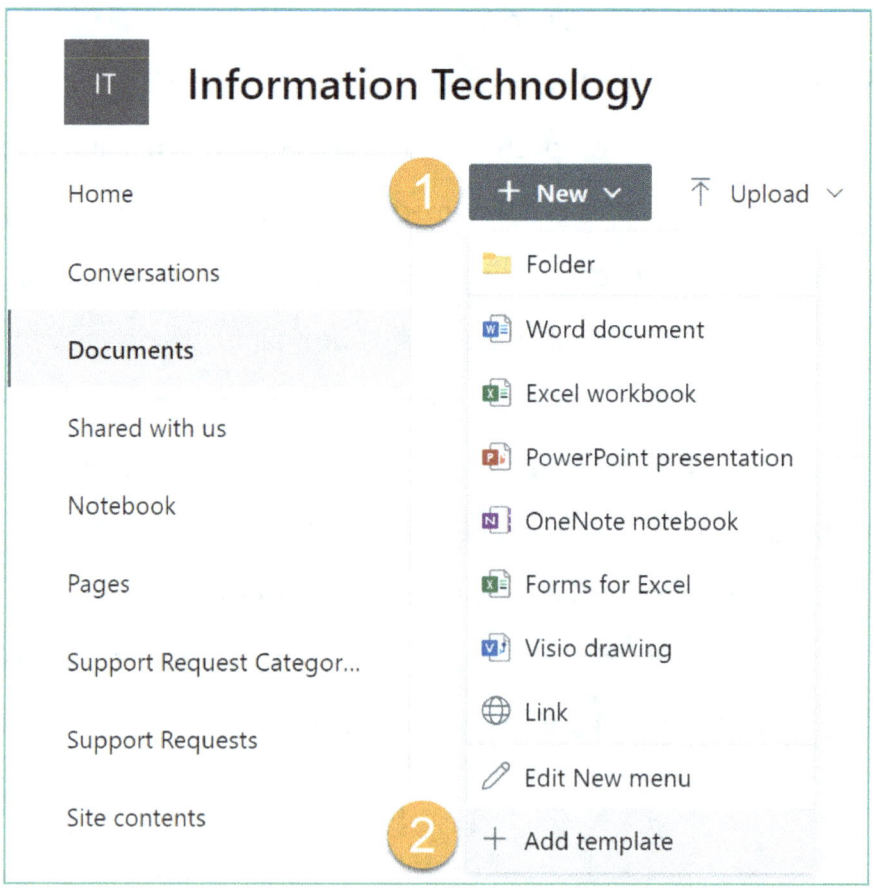

Figure 6 - Steps to add a document template to a document library

- **Content approval:** The city's quality checkpoint. Before content gets the green light, SharePoint's optional, built-in approval workflows can act as gatekeepers, ensuring accuracy, relevance, and professionalism.

SECURE COLLABORATION: YOUR DIGITAL SAFE HAVEN

In a city, while openness fosters interaction, security ensures peace of mind. SharePoint mirrors this duality, balancing collaboration with robust protection:

- **Share options:** In addition to owners (full control), members (edit), and visitors (read), you can share documents and folders individually with individuals or groups who may not have access to your site and its contents typically. This can be done easily using share links, or by granting direct access – both of these are available when you select **Share** next to a document. These links are your city's access badges. Control who steps into your space, who can contribute, and who can merely observe and whether or not these individuals should be able to share the content even further with others. This guarantees that sensitive information remains in trusted hands.

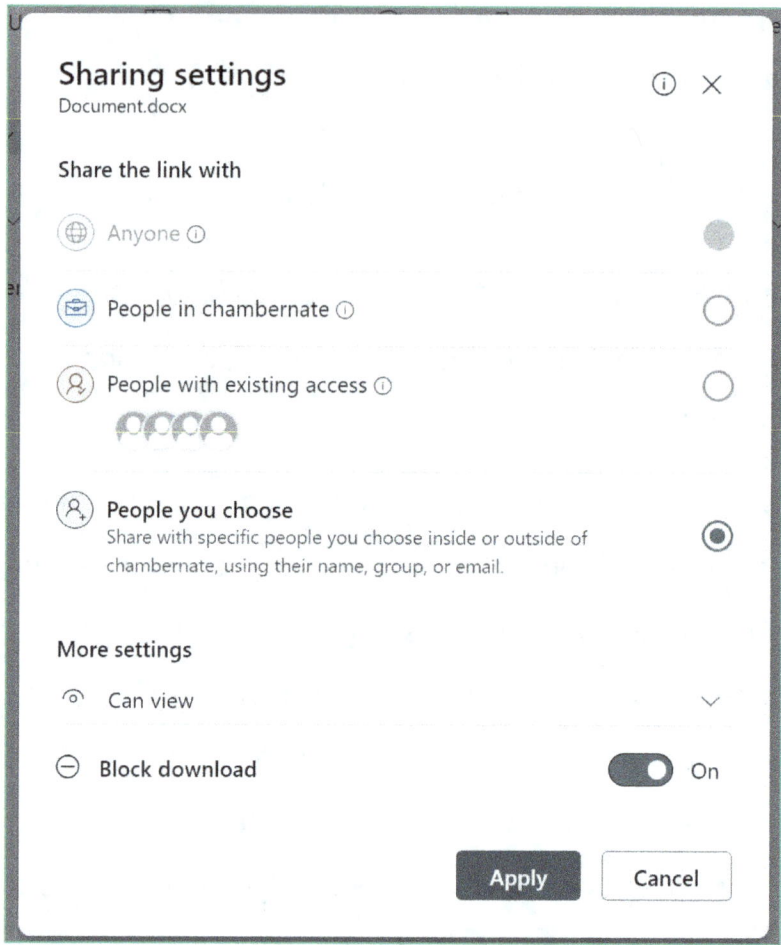

Figure 7 – Share link settings for a view-only, blocked download document

- **External sharing:** Akin to giving a visitor pass, SharePoint offers you the flexibility to bring external partners into the fold. Collaborate on shared goals, but with the reassurance of defined boundaries and monitored access. Note that your administrators and site owners control the availability of external sharing at an org-wide or site-by-site level.

With SharePoint's document collaboration tools in your arsenal, you're constructing more than just digital documents. You're laying down the bricks for a vibrant plaza where creativity is the currency, collaboration is the norm, and innovation is the inevitable outcome. As our exploration into SharePoint continues, watch this space transform into a nexus of communication, partnership, and unparalleled results.

E | EXPERIENCES

In the modern digital workplace, accessing SharePoint provides you with a wealth of information, collaboration, and productivity tools. Just as you would navigate through a physical space, understanding how to access SharePoint efficiently is the first step to making the most of its capabilities.

For letter **E**, we'll explore the various pathways to access SharePoint Online in different **experiences**, ensuring you're equipped to effortlessly navigate this powerful tool regardless of your context.

BROWSER ACCESS: YOUR PORTAL TO SHAREPOINT

Think of your web browser as the front door to SharePoint. Just like walking into a building, you can easily enter your organization's online workspace by opening your preferred browser and entering a

URL. If you haven't set up a bookmark, follow these steps to find SharePoint (and then consider bookmarking the site(s) you use most):

1. Open your web browser of choice, such as Edge, Firefox, or Chrome.

2. In the address bar, type *microsoft365.com* and press **Enter** to access all Microsoft 365 apps. You may need to first sign in with your work or school account if not already.

3. Once signed in, from the search bar or upper left app launcher (the nine-dot grid), find and select **SharePoint**.

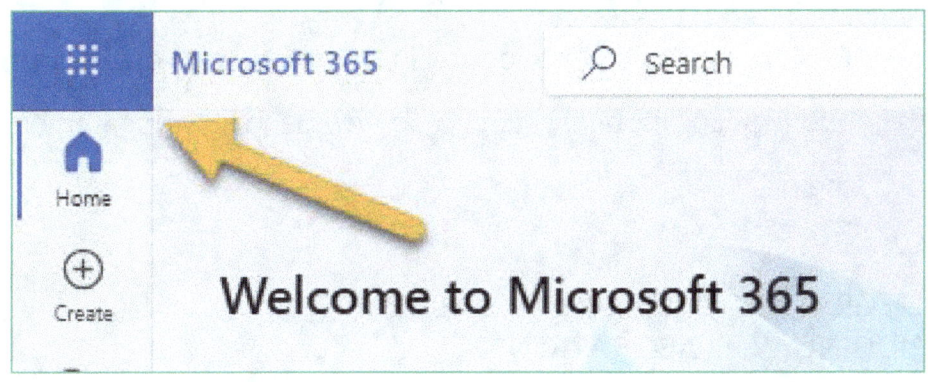

Figure 8 - App launcher location in the upper left corner of microsoft365.com

4. Finally, select the specific SharePoint site you wish to visit.

Keep in mind, you could also just use the search bar at the top of Microsoft365.com to search for the name of the specific site you wish to visit and skip steps 3-4.

MOBILE APP: SHAREPOINT ON THE MOVE

Just as a map guides you through a new city, the SharePoint mobile app keeps you connected to your digital workplace, even when you're away from your desk. To get started:

1. **Download the app:** Visit your device's app store and search for *SharePoint*. Download and install the official SharePoint app.
2. **Sign in:** Open the app and sign in using your organization's credentials (your work or school account).
3. **Explore content:** Once logged in, you can access documents and lists, collaborate, catch up on news, and stay updated on the go.

INTEGRATION WITH MICROSOFT TEAMS: BRIDGING COLLABORATION

Think of Microsoft Teams as a central meeting point in a busy city. It seamlessly integrates with SharePoint, allowing you to access content directly within Teams alongside your other important tools and content like Planner plans or third-party tools. You'll find SharePoint everywhere within Teams – it's the powerhouse behind all Files tabs in every team channel, after all. But you can also pin pages and sites as experiences within Teams and channels. More on this when we get to *M | Microsoft Teams and groups integration*.

KIOSK ACCESS: INFREQUENT FLYERS

For users with limited and specific access needs, SharePoint offers kiosk access. Like entering a specialized area in a building, kiosk access is tailored to certain tasks and users. Think of volunteers in a healthcare setting – they may not need all the typical employee resources for someone like a full-time nurse, so their kiosk-level access gives them just enough to learn about the organization, complete their shift paperwork, and get back to volunteering. To understand kiosk access:

- **Learn about kiosk access:** Check with your IT department to see if your organization uses kiosk access and what it offers.
- **Understand kiosk capabilities:** Kiosk access might limit features, but it can be ideal for specific tasks or user roles.

Understanding the various experiences (browsers, mobile apps, kiosk, and Teams integrations) helps you be ready to navigate SharePoint with confidence and make the most of its capabilities. Accessing SharePoint is your entry point to a world of collaboration, information sharing, and productivity.

F | FORMS INTEGRATION

COLLECT AND ANALYZE DATA

For letter **F**, let's explore the integration of **Microsoft Forms** within SharePoint. Forms is a versatile tool to create surveys, quizzes, and data collection forms. This integration enhances user engagement, simplifies data collection, and empowers users of varying technical abilities to gather valuable insights.

VERSATILITY IN CREATION: DESIGNING INTERACTIVE FORMS

Microsoft Forms is a hub for creating interactive forms and surveys that can be distributed within your organization (as a link, a SharePoint web part embed, or a Teams channel tab) and even outside your organization for anonymous data collection if external sharing is enabled by your admin. Here's a closer look at how Forms enhances engagement:

- **Microsoft Forms web part:** The Microsoft Forms web part allows you to embed forms directly into your SharePoint pages, offering a seamless experience for users to provide their input without leaving the site or toggling between resources. *Figure 9* shows how this might look when placed among other web parts like a Quick chart web part and an image.

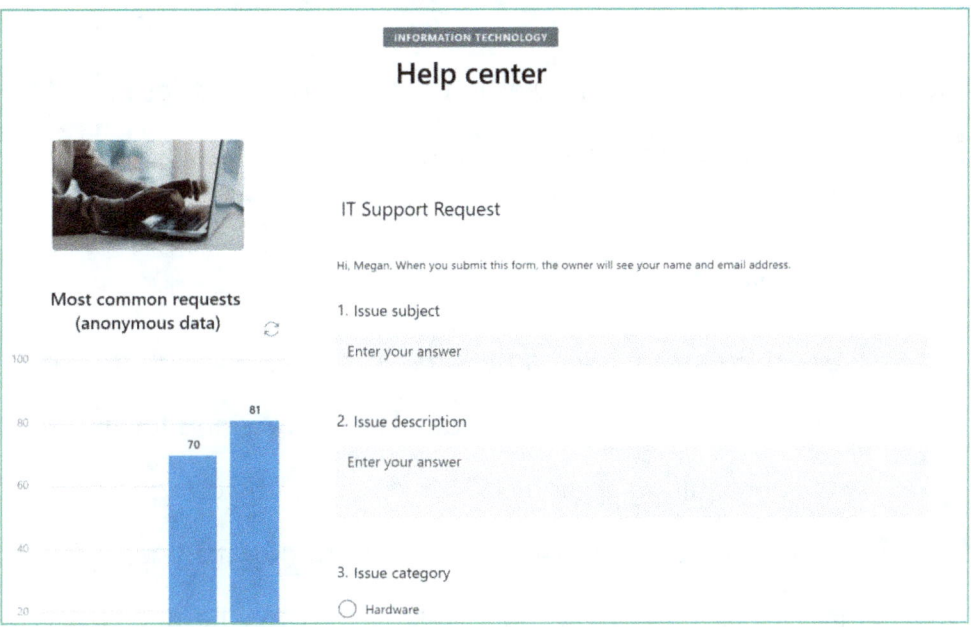

Figure 9 - A Microsoft Forms web part embedded on a SharePoint page alongside other web parts

- **Site-independent:** Forms built in Microsoft Forms can be embedded on multiple team sites. This means you can gather specific data within the context of different projects or teams, enhancing data relevance and analysis, while managing the responses and form design from a single, central location. All the web part requires is the form's response collection URL which remains the same from one site to another. Just be sure your form's settings allow everyone in your organization to participate.

SIMPLICITY IN USAGE: ACCESSIBLE TO ALL

The creation of forms and quizzes in Microsoft Forms is designed to be a user-friendly and accessible experience for a a broad spectrum of users, regardless of technical expertise. Here's how it caters to various user levels:

- **Ease of creation:** Microsoft Forms provides a straightforward interface (point and click) for building surveys and forms without requiring coding skills or complex customization. It offers a variety of question types and even branching logic, making it simple to design forms tailored to your needs.
- **Accessibility over complexity:** Microsoft Forms ensures that users with varying technical abilities can actively participate. Instead of delving into complex options like JSON customization of a SharePoint list form or getting into Power Apps development, you can quickly create powerful forms in

Microsoft Forms that suit your requirements and offer easy maintenance over their lifetime.

INTEGRATION FOR ACTION: EMPOWERING DECISIONS

Much like city events influencing community decisions, the data collected through Microsoft Forms within SharePoint empowers informed decision-making within your organization. Here's how it translates into action:

- **Data collection for insights:** Imagine this as gathering community opinions. Microsoft Forms gathers responses and stores them directly on your SharePoint team site, making it easy for teams to access and analyze the data collected.
- **Sharing insights:** Similar to sharing findings from city surveys, you can share a summarized results page with others in just a few clicks, without revealing too many specific details like names and email addresses. Imagine each question getting its own summary pie or bar chart in a scrollable web page.

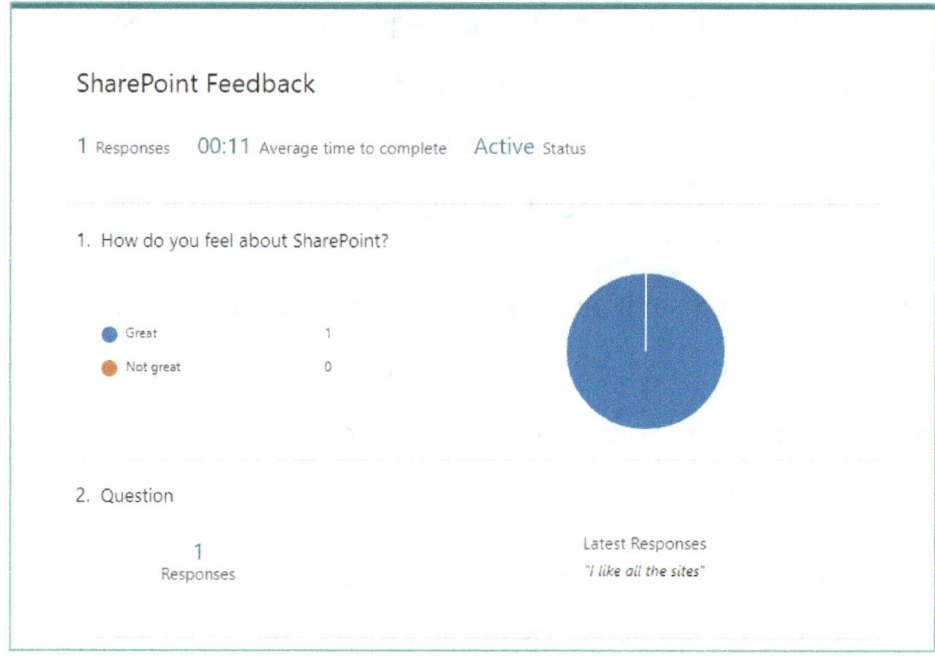

SharePoint Feedback

1 Responses   00:11 Average time to complete   Active Status

1. How do you feel about SharePoint?

🔵 Great   1
🟠 Not great   0

2. Question

1
Responses

Latest Responses
"I like all the sites"

Figure 10 - Example of a summary page of a form's results

- **Sharing the work:** If your form belongs to a Microsoft 365 group or, in other words, was created in a specific group as opposed to just within your own account, your teammates have access to edit the form and review responses at any time. This enables collaboration and ensures that relevant stakeholders can access and utilize the collected data for informed actions.

By utilizing Microsoft Forms' integration within SharePoint, you're essentially creating a connection that engages users, simplifies data collection, and empowers decision-makers.

G | GRANULAR PERMISSIONS

For letter **G**, let's delve into the intricate world of **granular permissions** within SharePoint. Just as a city assigns different staff positions and leaders to ensure the smooth functioning of its various departments, SharePoint empowers you to wield precise control over access and permissions, aligning them with users' roles and requirements.

PRECISION ACCESS: ROLE-BASED PERMISSIONS

SharePoint's granular permissions enable you to assign specific roles and access levels to users. Here's a closer look at this role-based access:

- **Role-based access:** SharePoint allows you to assign roles and permissions to individuals, ensuring they access only what's relevant and appropriate for them to access. At a most basic level, owners control everything (permissions and content), members edit and contribute (just content), and visitors read. Every site has a SharePoint group called **Site visitors**, which is different from the Microsoft 365 group membership that only has owners and members. When sharing a team site (**Settings | Site permissions**), you'll notice you can add members to a (Microsoft 365) group, or **Share site only**. When you choose **Share site only**, you can give a user **Read** access which adds them to this unique visitors group.

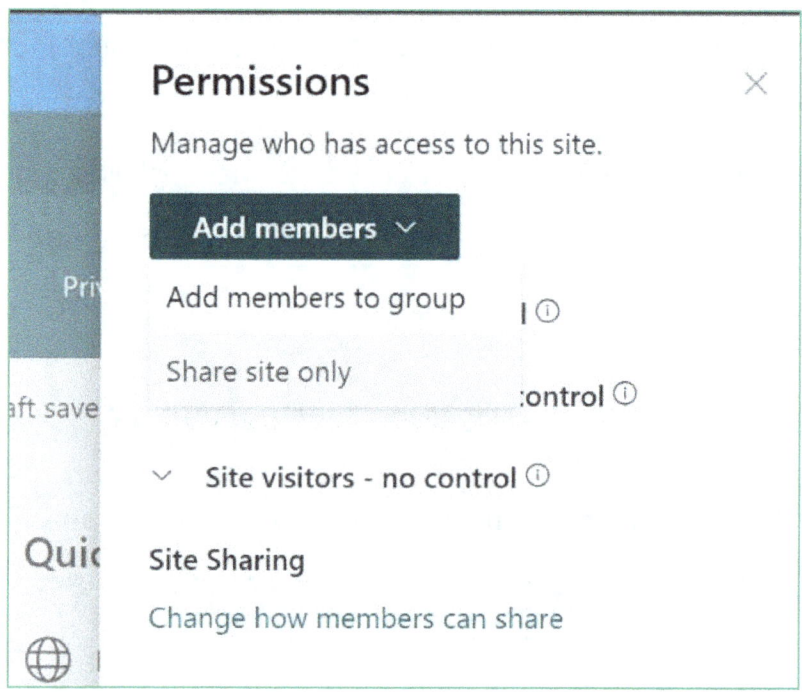

Figure 11 - Information shown when adding new members and/owners to a team site

- **Permission inheritance:** Think of this as maintaining consistency across city districts. SharePoint allows you to apply permissions at different levels—site, library, or item. But by default, whatever your site's permissions are (owners, members, and visitors) will trickle down through all lists, libraries, folders, files, and items on the site. This inheritance ensures that permissions applied at higher levels are automatically inherited by sub-items, maintaining a structured access hierarchy.

- **Unique/broken permissions:** While not typically considered a best practice, SharePoint does allow you to break inheritance or, in other words, make one list, library, folder, etc. on a site have permissions that are different than the rest of the site's default permissions. Perhaps one document library on a site should only be seen by site owners. This ensures that users access only the information that's relevant to their roles, without overexposing sensitive data or creating site sprawl by creating additional sites or groups just for a single library need.

SharePoint's granular permissions help you collaborate securely within and beyond your organization. Here are some features that enhance security and collaboration confidence:

- **External sharing:** This lets you grant temporary and controlled access to specific content for external users, such as partners, vendors, or clients. Note that your admin and individual site owners can restrict this ability, so it may be disabled.

- **Limited access:** This lets you provide guest passes to designated areas, while restricting access to other parts of the site. This protects data privacy and prevents unauthorized exploration.

- **Conditional access:** This lets you set entry requirements, such as geographic locations or device compliance, before external users can access your shared content.

- **Multi-Factor Authentication (MFA):** This adds an extra layer of security to external user logins by verifying their identity. This ensures that only the intended collaborators can access your content.

SharePoint's robust permissions options allow you to be both the expander and the architect of your digital city. Use external sharing for collaboration beyond your organization while safeguarding content. Utilize granular permissions to control access, aligning collaboration with security based on user roles. These permissions promote seamless collaboration and information sharing across your digital landscape.

H | HUB SITES: CENTRALIZED COLLABORATION

CREATE A STRUCTURE OF CONNECTED CONTENT

SharePoint's hub sites stand as a testament to the platform's commitment to fostering centralized collaboration. Echoing the principles of a well-organized city where services and resources are centralized for efficiency, hub sites in SharePoint achieve a similar feat in the digital realm. By acting as a centralized hub for various associated sites, they streamline collaboration, data sharing, and user navigation.

CENTRALIZED COLLABORATION: AN EPICENTER OF ACTIVITY

At the heart of every city lies its bustling squares and central districts. Similarly, SharePoint's hub sites serve as the nucleus of activity for all connected sites, offering:

- **Site organization:** Hub sites act as pivotal points, bringing together related team and communication sites. This alignment simplifies the user journey, providing clarity and easy access to information.
- **Unified identity:** Hub sites are not just about content organization; they are about creating a recognizable digital space. By offering consistent navigation and branding, they reinforce a sense of familiarity and trust among users.

UNIFIED INFORMATION SHARING: THE BEATING HEART OF DATA DISPERSION

A well-informed citizenry drives a city's progress. SharePoint's hub sites play a similar informing role by centralizing data dissemination:

- **Broadcast central:** Much like how a city's announcement system disseminates key updates, hub sites enable you to broadcast news and essential announcements to all connected sites.

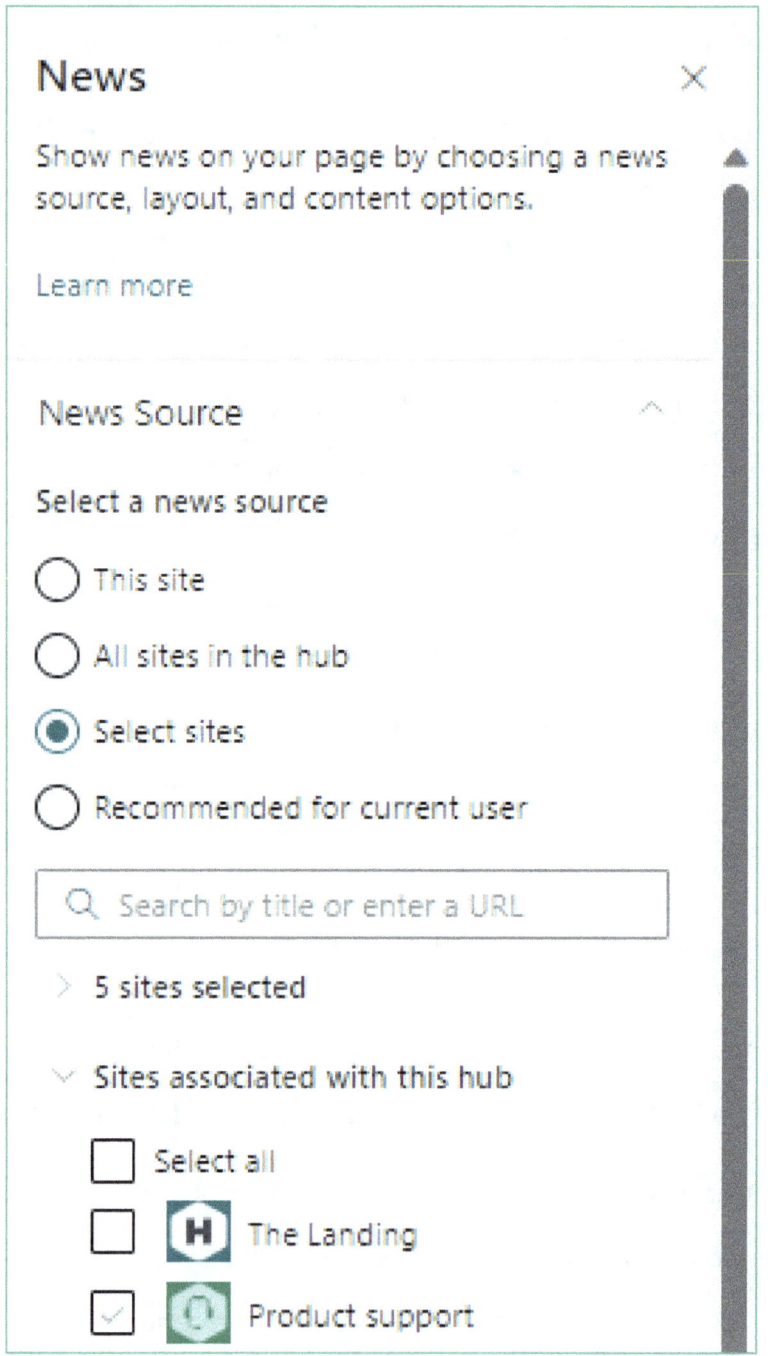

Figure 12 - Settings for the SharePoint news web part showing hub options

- **Resource repository:** Cities thrive when resources are shared and accessible. Similarly, hub sites store shared documents, templates, and resources, ensuring users have everything they need at their fingertips.

STREAMLINED CONTENT DISCOVERY: NAVIGATING THE DIGITAL CITYSCAPE

Navigational aids in a city, be it signboards or maps, ensure residents and visitors find their way. In the vast expanse of SharePoint, hub sites play this navigational role:

- **Content aggregation:** Acting as a centralized bulletin board, hub sites pull in content such as news and events from all linked sites, giving users an overview of what's happening across the board.
- **Optimized search:** Time is of the essence. Hub sites enhance search functionalities, allowing users to efficiently find content across the hub ecosystem (hub, child hubs, and associated sites) without the need to hop between individual sites.

Hub sites are connections where collaboration, resource sharing, and efficient navigation are the order of the day. As you continue your exploration of SharePoint, it becomes evident how these hubs are not just organizational tools but pivotal elements in constructing a cohesive, user-friendly digital workspace.

I | INTRANET PERSONALIZATION

CREATE A DIGITAL BRAND

SharePoint's ability to personalize the intranet experience is akin to how a city offers diverse neighborhoods tailored to the unique preferences or identities of its residents. This ensures a user-centric approach, where information and resources perfectly align with and reflect individual roles and interests.

TAILORED INFORMATION: PERSONALIZED PATHWAYS IN A DIGITAL REALM

Cities come alive with varied landscapes and districts, catering to different residents' lifestyles and preferences. Similarly, SharePoint's intranet personalization creates a custom experience for each user:

- **Personalized news:** Like a city's newspaper that offers local updates, each SharePoint site delivers news articles and resources tailored to its membership and, if configured, audience targeted as well, providing pertinent updates that truly matter.

- **Recommended resources:** Think of this feature as a personal city guide, handpicked just for you. SharePoint intelligently suggests documents, sites, and news based on individual activity and past preferences, streamlining the process of content discovery and making it more valuable. These recommendations/suggestions can appear in web parts, the SharePoint start page, and other locations throughout Microsoft 365.

ROLE-BASED EXPERIENCE: A CUSTOM-BUILT DIGITAL ENVIRONMENT

Every city has designated zones for different activities: business districts, residential areas, recreational parks, and more. SharePoint's intranet personalization reflects this by tailoring experiences according to user roles:

- **Targeted content:** In the same way a city planner zones areas for specific purposes, SharePoint can showcase content designed for specific user groups. This ensures the information presented is not only relevant but also engaging. Content creators configure audience targeting in web part settings, news settings, navigation links, and other locations where supported.

- **Followed content:** Similar to how one might have preferred spots in a city, users can follow or bookmark specific documents, sites, and news in SharePoint. This creates a personalized feed, ensuring they stay more easily connected to areas of prime interest.

EFFICIENT ENGAGEMENT: OPTIMIZED ROUTES THROUGH THE DIGITAL CITYSCAPE

The best city designs minimize congestion and ensure fluidity of movement. In a similar vein, SharePoint's intranet personalization – particularly when it comes to designing navigation menus and features – facilitates effortless user wayfinding and engagement:

- **Quick links:** Just as cities have fast lanes and shortcuts to avoid traffic, you can create quick links web parts, giving users direct routes to vital sites and resources.
- **Dynamic pages:** SharePoint's dynamic pages adapt their content based on user identities, roles, and interactions, ensuring a continually engaging and relevant experience. This is sometimes from audience targeting settings, item-level

permissions on lists or library web parts, intelligent content suggestions, etc. which personalize the page's web parts for each user. Notice in *Figure 13* how graphic web parts, like hero and highlighted content web parts, help bring an intranet page to life in just a glance.

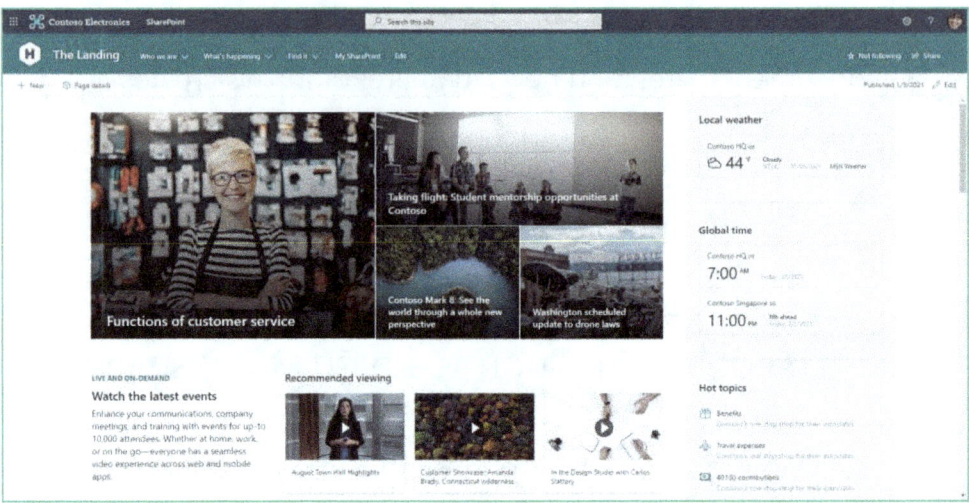

Figure 13 - Example of a SharePoint communication site using Microsoft's The Landing template

Incorporating SharePoint's intranet personalization techniques is like being the mayor of a digital city, where every street, building, and public space can be molded to best serve its residents. This tailored approach not only elevates user satisfaction but also amplifies efficiency.

J | JUNCTIONS OF DISCOVERY WITH VIVA TOPICS

Viva Topics, integrated within SharePoint, introduces the sophisticated technique of journey mapping to the digital information space, reminiscent of charting pathways through a complex city. Leveraging AI, Viva Topics guides users through intricate networks of themes, experts, and resources, streamlining the process of information discovery.

AI-POWERED NAVIGATION: YOUR KNOWLEDGE COMPASS

Just as a seasoned tour guide can illuminate hidden gems in a bustling metropolis, Viva Topics shines a light on relevant content within SharePoint:

- **Related Topics:** By using AI, Viva Topics identifies and highlights connected areas of interest, simplifying your search and making information easily accessible.
- **Expertise Discovery:** Imagine connecting with a local historian when exploring a city's ancient quarter. In the same vein, when a user stumbles upon a term or topic in SharePoint, Viva Topics introduces them to domain experts, promoting direct collaboration and ensuring access to the most accurate and pertinent information.

TOPIC CARDS: YOUR DIGITAL SIGNPOSTS

Strolling through a historic city, travelers often encounter signs offering insights into landmarks. Viva Topics employs this idea with its dynamic topic cards:

- **Topic Overviews:** Just as a signpost provides a snapshot of a monument's history, topic cards encapsulate the crux of subjects. They provide concise details about a topic, its relevance, and pathways for in-depth exploration.
- **Connected Resources:** Just as a city guide might point out nearby attractions, topic cards not only present a topic but also highlight associated documents, dialogues, and expert channels. This ensures that users are always a step away from a comprehensive understanding.

With Viva Topics as your digital companion within SharePoint, navigating the vast information terrain becomes as intuitive as traversing a well-mapped city. The tool doesn't merely simplify access; it acts as a catalyst, accelerating the discovery process and enhancing collaboration. By harnessing its power, organizations can foster a culture where knowledge flows effortlessly, promoting continuous learning and collaboration.

K | KNOWLEDGE SHARING WITH VIVA CONNECTIONS

BRING SHAREPOINT CLOSER

When we think of SharePoint and its growing functionalities, Viva Connections emerges as a stellar innovation in the landscape of digital collaboration. Envision an expansive city with its information hubs, bustling squares, and digital billboards; Viva Connections mirrors this dynamism, offering a centralized and personalized portal for every essential company resource, announcement, and update. It gives us letter **K, Knowledge sharing**.

DASHBOARD: YOUR DIGITAL TOOLSET

The Viva Connections dashboard plays this role in our digital city:

- **Dynamic Cards:** Think of cards as interactive booths or kiosks in a city square, each serving a unique purpose. They are interactive, allowing employees to complete job-specific tasks such as clocking in for a shift, accessing training and resources, accessing pay systems and information, or even booking travel accommodation – these cards and integrations are determined and set up by your administrators. This can be viewed on mobile or desktop; an idea of the mobile layout with tasks, shifts, and approvals cards can be seen in *Figure 14.*

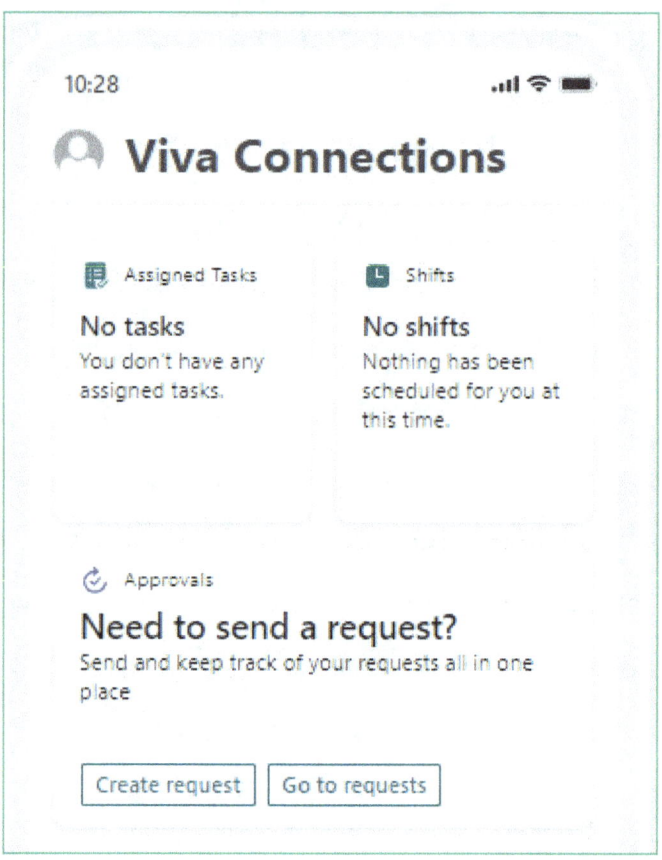

Figure 14 - Possible mobile layout for cards in Viva Connections

- **Adaptive Nature:** Powered by adaptive cards and the SharePoint Framework (SPFx), these cards offer a low-code solution, integrating your essential business apps right into the dashboard. Imagine these as customizable stalls, tailored to meet specific needs.

- **Integration with SharePoint:** In combination with SharePoint home sites, the dashboard can be further customized and expanded using SPFx web parts and extensions.

MOBILE EXPERIENCE: KNOWLEDGE IN YOUR POCKET

The modern city dweller is always on the move, relying on mobile tools and apps to navigate their urban environment. Viva Connections, with its robust mobile functionalities, ensures you're equipped with all the necessary tools for this digital age:

- **Mobile app:** Just as essential city-based apps inform residents of everything from traffic updates to local events, Viva Connections' app inside Microsoft Teams is a digital companion par excellence. Whether you're commuting, traveling, or working remotely, it keeps company news, essential resources, and announcements right at your fingertips a tap away from your chats and channels.

In the bustling streets of our metaphorical city, newsstands and billboards keep citizens informed. The Viva Connections feed embodies this essence:

- **Targeted Updates:** Delivering the right updates to the right individuals, it integrates seamlessly with Viva Engage, SharePoint news, and Stream. It's as if every billboard was tailored to the viewer, displaying news and updates that matter most to them.

- **Personalization:** Based on post-level targeting of groups employees belong to, the feed caters both to centralized corporate communications and democratized news scenarios.

- **Engagement anywhere:** It's not just confined to the city center. The feed is available in the Viva Connections Teams app and can also be embedded on SharePoint sites using its specific web part.

Using Viva Connections within SharePoint is akin to having a bird's-eye view of a digital cityscape. It's not just about functionality; it's about experiencing a transformative digital journey. As we continue to traverse SharePoint's vast landscapes, tools like Viva Connections stand out, emphasizing the importance of knowledge dissemination and the sense of community. Through such tools, organizations are not only connected but are also brought closer together.

L

L | LISTS REINVENTED

For letter **L**, let's explore the transformative nature of SharePoint's **Lists** – or Microsoft Lists – a pivotal component that has been reinvented to amplify user experience. Envisioning a city's intricate systems and services, Microsoft Lists provides an analogous platform, orchestrating myriad facets of information and processes with finesse.

BUILDING BLOCKS: FOUNDATIONAL STRUCTURES

Let's dive into the capabilities of lists:

- **Detailed data categorization:** Like a city's directory, lists enable the categorization of vast amounts of data, streamlining accessibility and clarity. They can be organized in multiple ways using multiple views per list. You choose which columns and column types exist, giving you maximum flexibility.

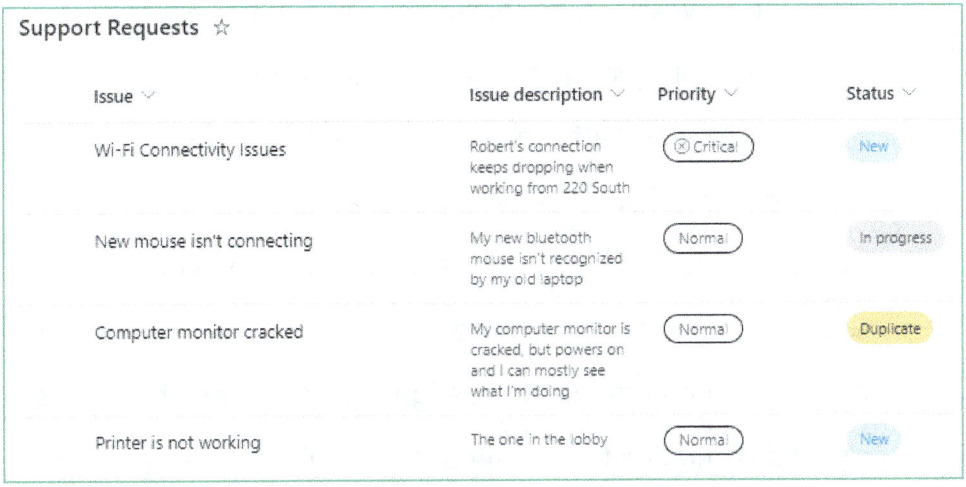
Support Requests ☆

Issue	Issue description	Priority	Status
Wi-Fi Connectivity Issues	Robert's connection keeps dropping when working from 220 South	Critical	New
New mouse isn't connecting	My new bluetooth mouse isn't recognized by my old laptop	Normal	In progress
Computer monitor cracked	My computer monitor is cracked, but powers on and I can mostly see what I'm doing	Normal	Duplicate
Printer is not working	The one in the lobby	Normal	New

Figure 15 - A Support Requests list example with multiple columns

- **Flexible views:** Imagine this as viewing the city from different vantage points. Lists allow the creation of diverse views based on filters, sorting, and grouping, providing the desired perspective to data. You can think of these as different ways of reporting on your site's data. Examples include grouping list items by department, those assigned to you (dynamic per user), or filtering by fiscal year so you'll have one view per year.
- **Synchronized collaboration:** Lists facilitate seamless collaboration, allowing multiple stakeholders to interact and contribute in a list at the same time. One user may be

updating an existing request being tracked in a list, while another is adding a whole new one.

- **Integration with Power Platform:** Think of this as a city's integrated public systems. Lists seamlessly integrate with Microsoft Power Platform, amplifying automation, and app creation capabilities. Consider a scenario where an issue tracker list automatically notifies an assignee of a new issue submitted via a form customized with Power Apps, and Power Automate then reminds the assignee to complete it until it is marked complete, then notifies the original requestor.

INTEGRATED TEMPLATES: READY-MADE FRAMEWORKS

Drawing an analogy to a city's modular buildings, SharePoint's list templates function as ready-made frameworks tailored for distinct use cases:

- **Travel requests** Envision this as a central place where submitted travel requests are monitored, updated, and reported upon. It automatically calculates travel duration, and can be used with Power Automate to request approval prior to being processed.
- **Asset tracking:** Use this template to maintain a record of IT hardware assets, their condition, and assignment status.

ADVANCED CUSTOMIZATION: YOUR CITY, YOUR RULES

Lists in SharePoint can be tailored to meet specific organizational nuances:

- **Integration with Power Automate:** Integrate lists with Power Automate to establish data flow, facilitate approvals, send reminders, and more, automating tasks and procedures based on triggers and conditions.
- **Data validation:** These are quality checks. Incorporate validation rules to ensure data integrity, enhancing reliability.
- **Advanced security:** Aligning with the security protocols of a city, implement user permissions at both list and item levels, ensuring data safety and controlled access. Those who should review can review, while those who should update can update.

Embracing the robustness of the reinvented Lists in SharePoint is akin to mastering the dynamics of a thriving city. With structured data management, templates, and advanced customization, you're steering your digital landscape to be more coherent, dynamic, and user-centric. As we continue our journey through SharePoint, recognize that it's not just about managing data but about curating experiences, fostering collaborations, and elevating efficiency in the digital realm.

M | MICROSOFT TEAMS AND GROUPS INTEGRATION

UNDERSTAND THE CORE OF TEAM SITES

For letter **M**, we're diving deep into the harmonious interplay between **Microsoft Teams** and SharePoint. These entities represent the confluence of two digital territories within your organizational universe, collaboratively bringing you a platform for robust communication alongside content orchestration.

MEETING OF TWO GIANTS: SHAREPOINT AND TEAMS

Visualize Microsoft Teams as the bustling metropolis, buzzing with discussions, interactions, and instant decision-making. On the other side, envision SharePoint as the underlying infrastructure, the vast network of roads, libraries, and archives that give the metropolis its depth and substance. This synergy offers numerous avenues:

- **Integrated permissions:** Within the Teams environment, permissions and membership sync with SharePoint. This means when you add someone to a Team, they receive the necessary permissions in that team's supporting SharePoint site to access the team's relevant files and documents.

- **Tabs for quick access:** SharePoint pages or lists can be added as a tab in Teams, like that shown in *Figure 16*, ensuring that important sites or lists are just a click away within your team.

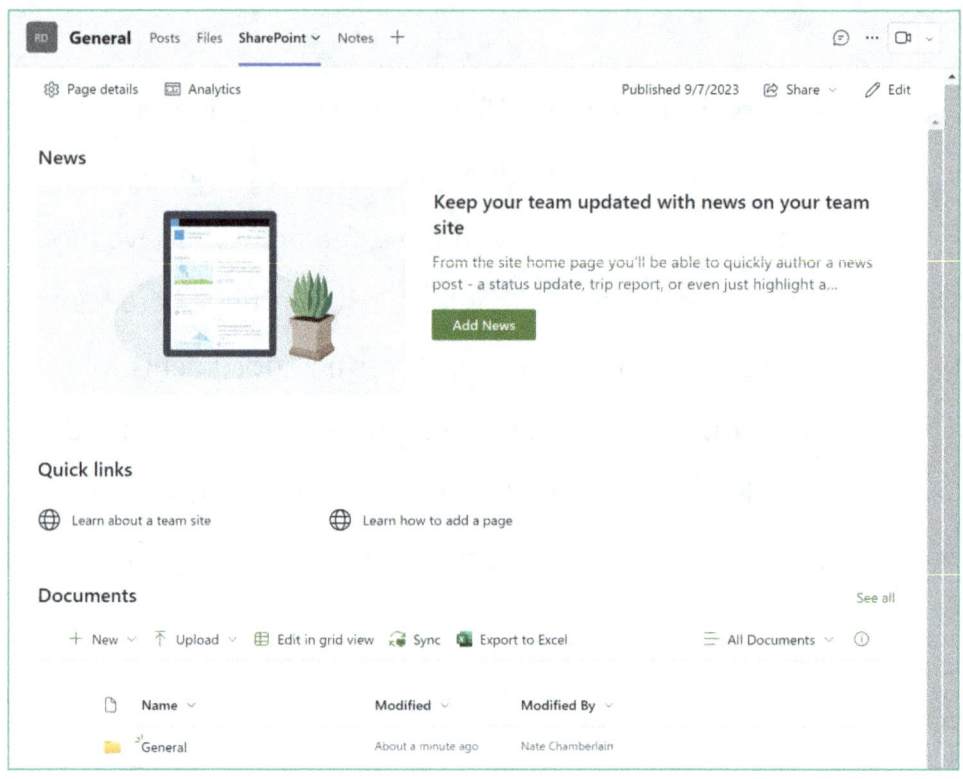

Figure 16 - A team's SharePoint site's home page as a tab in their team's General channel

- **Notifications and activity:** Activity in SharePoint, like edits to a shared document, can trigger notifications in Teams, ensuring that team members are immediately informed of any updates.

NAVIGATING THE DIGITAL TERRAIN: WHEN TO OPT FOR ONE OR BOTH

Drawing parallels with city planning, think of SharePoint and Teams as different zones. Sometimes you need the quiet order of a library (SharePoint) and sometimes the lively atmosphere of a town square (Teams):

- **SharePoint as your library:** Ideal for scenarios where structured data storage, historical data archives, and a broad organization of content is paramount. For example, when deploying a corporate-wide announcement or a repository of annual reports.
- **SharePoint & Teams - The lively town square:** You can't have Teams without SharePoint, so we discuss these as a pair. For project-based work, where real-time communication and immediate access to shared files are essential, this integration shines. Teams bring the interaction (chats, calls, and meetings) while SharePoint offers the structured content and foundation.

EVOLVING YOUR DIGITAL LANDSCAPE: ENHANCING SHAREPOINT WITH TEAMS

Think of taking an old city district and adding a modern touch, transforming it into a dynamic hub:

- **Seamless transition:** If you have been primarily using SharePoint, you can easily enhance your site with the dynamic capabilities of Teams. It's about combining the depth of SharePoint with the agility of Teams.

- **Centralized communication:** The integration ensures that all discussions about a document or project stored in SharePoint can happen right within Teams. It reduces the need to switch platforms and keeps the context intact.

- **Unified search experience:** Search across both platforms at once. Whether you're looking for a document from SharePoint or a chat from Teams, a unified search ensures you find what you need quickly whether it's a chat message you sent or a news post from HR.

- **Integrated apps & workflows:** Using Microsoft Power Automate, you can integrate your other group apps like Planner with SharePoint to automate workflows, even triggering actions in Teams like conversation posts based on updates in SharePoint.

As our digital exploration progresses, it becomes evident how Microsoft Teams and SharePoint's amalgamation acts as a force multiplier. By leveraging this alliance, organizations can craft a digital ecosystem that's not just efficient but also intuitive, meeting the varied demands of modern-day collaboration and content management. It's akin to a city where historical archives seamlessly blend with bustling squares, offering both depth and dynamism.

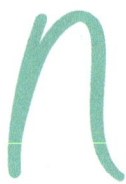

N | NEWS AND PAGES: CRAFTING ENGAGING CONTENT IN SHAREPOINT

INFORM AND CONSUME

In the evolving digital age, the way we consume information and communicate narratives has transformed. For letter **N**, we'll delve into SharePoint's **News and pages**, the linchpins of content dissemination and presentation in your digital workspace.

SHAREPOINT PAGES: YOUR CANVAS FOR CONTENT

SharePoint Pages are akin to blank canvases waiting for an artist's touch. These pages are where you present structured content, tailor experiences, and guide users through your digital space.

- **Dynamic layouts:** Craft and organize your content using various layouts, ensuring your message is conveyed effectively and elegantly.

- **Web parts:** Enrich your pages by embedding interactive elements such as videos, forms, and graphs.

- **Responsive design:** SharePoint pages adapt to the device they're viewed on, be it a desktop, tablet, or mobile.

SHAREPOINT NEWS: YOUR DIGITAL BULLETIN

SharePoint News acts as the heartbeat of your organization's updates. It's where timely announcements, stories, and highlights come alive.

- **Timely announcements:** Share organizational updates, upcoming events, and key milestones to keep your team informed.

- **Multimedia integration:** Make your news articles visually appealing with images, videos, and links.

- **Engage and interact:** Foster a culture of interaction by enabling comments and likes on news posts, allowing real-time feedback and discussions.

The power of SharePoint's content management lies in the seamless integration of news and pages:

- **Embed the news web part in pages:** Highlight important news articles within your SharePoint pages, ensuring essential updates don't go unnoticed.

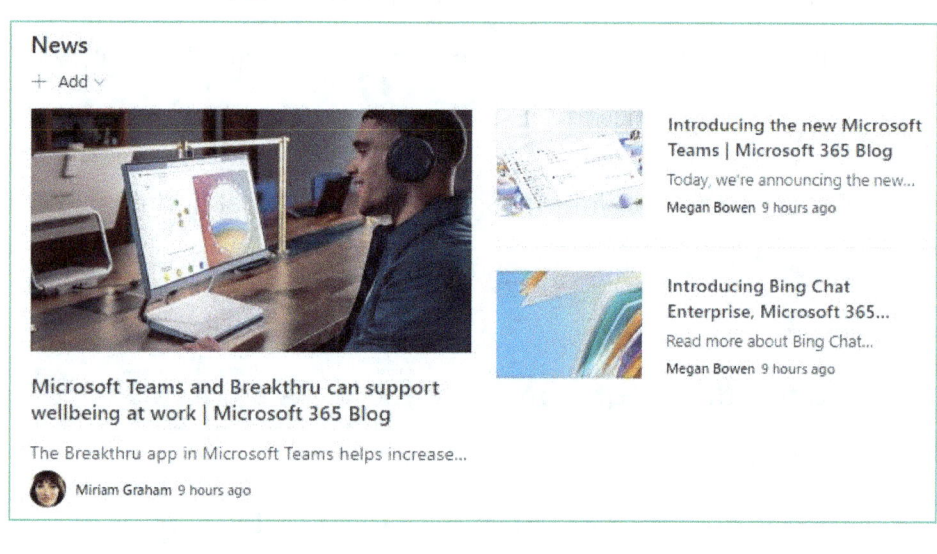

Figure 17 - A news web part featuring 3 news links from Microsoft 365 Blog

- **Consistent branding:** Ensure both your news articles and pages echo your organization's branding and ethos. Also consider consistent header images, page layouts, etc. for similar types of news like system maintenance announcements, holiday procedure updates, etc.

- **Tailored experience:** Utilize audience targeting to display relevant news and content to specific groups or individuals.

In the realm of SharePoint, News and Pages are the keystones of effective communication. As you navigate through these features, you'll discover the potential to shape, inform, and engage your audience in novel ways. By mastering the art of crafting compelling pages and timely news updates, you're not just sharing information; you're telling a story, fostering a dynamic community, and cultivating a connected digital environment.

O | ONEDRIVE INTEGRATION

In our exploration of SharePoint, the letter **O** brings us to **OneDrive**, its trusty partner for individual file storage. Picture this: In the sprawling cityscape of SharePoint, OneDrive is akin to your private storage locker, safeguarding your personal treasures.

A SPACE OF YOUR OWN WITHIN A COLLABORATIVE UNIVERSE: THE ONEDRIVE PROMISE

While SharePoint is a bustling digital marketplace of collaboration, OneDrive offers a serene, private corner for each user. This individual space amidst the hubbub is what makes OneDrive indispensable:

- **Your individual files, anytime, anywhere:** Much like a city dweller accessing their locker, with OneDrive, your essential files are at your fingertips—be it at the office, during travel, or while working from home.

- **Find your files with ease:** Think of OneDrive's search as your digital detective. With its precision, sifting through files is swift and straightforward, saving you precious moments.

- **Automatic safekeeping:** Picture a safety deposit box that self-updates. OneDrive ensures your crucial local computer files, from desktop to pictures, are automatically backed up.

- **Solo yet social:** While OneDrive is your individual space, it isn't a secluded island. Seamlessly integrated with SharePoint, transitioning from private tasks to team projects is a breeze.

WHY ONEDRIVE STANDS OUT: BEYOND TRADITIONAL STORAGE

When compared to standard storage solutions, OneDrive shines with features that go beyond:

- **Stay alert with ransomware protection:** Visualize a vigilant security guard for your digital city. OneDrive notifies you of potential ransomware threats, letting you revert your data to a safer time.

- **Access files as needed:** It's like having instant access portals across your city. Fetch files when you wish, without clogging up device memory.

- **Extra secure personal vault:** Envision a fortified chamber in your storage locker. This is where you can stow away sensitive data, accessed only through unique identity checks, like a fingerprint or security code.

ONEDRIVE AND SHAREPOINT: THE PERFECT INTERSECTION

Venturing further into the OneDrive-SharePoint synergy, it's a harmonious dance of private and public spaces in our digital city. Boundaries exist, but transitions are fluid. The objective? Crafting a balanced digital realm where personal tasks effortlessly weave into team collaborations.

In this digital era, OneDrive's role within SharePoint exemplifies the balance between collective teamwork and individual space.

P | PROCESS AUTOMATION

P is for **Process automation**. In the modern digital workspace, the need to reduce manual, repetitive tasks has never been higher. SharePoint stands at the forefront of this efficiency drive, offering a versatile range of tools designed to automate many common business processes without the need for advanced tech skills.

AUTOMATE | RULES FOR LISTS AND LIBRARIES:

SharePoint offers an intuitive way to streamline tasks with its **Automate | Rules** feature for lists and libraries. This allows even the most non-technical users to establish automation directly within their lists or libraries in less than a minute.

- Notify team members when a new document is added to a shared library.
- Automatically set metadata (column values) for items based on conditions (e.g., marking an item as *High Priority* if its due date is within a week).
- Track items and create alerts when a list item remains unchanged for a set period.

SETTING IT UP

1. Navigate to the desired SharePoint list or library.
2. On the toolbar, select **Automate** and then **Rules**.

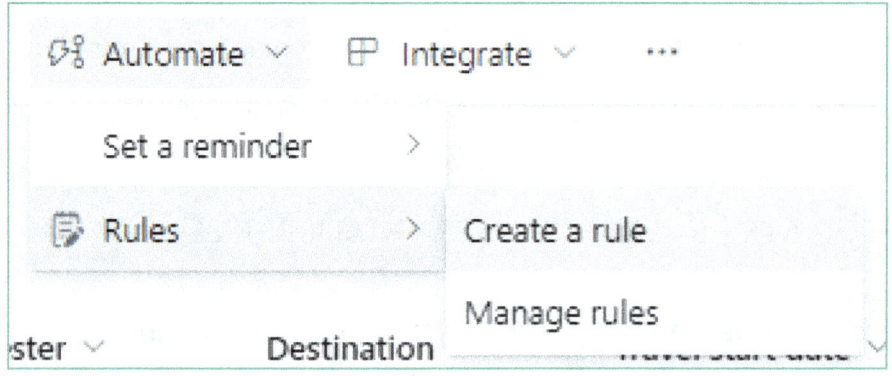

Figure 18 - Automate | Rules option for a SharePoint list or library

3. Define your triggers (like an item being added) and actions (like sending an email).

INTEGRATION | POWER AUTOMATE | CREATE FLOW

Harnessing the synergy between SharePoint and Power Automate, users can effortlessly establish more intricate automations. The embedded integration means users can design and deploy flows without navigating away from their SharePoint environments.

POTENTIAL USES

- Create a feedback loop by automatically sending a survey after a document gets approved.
- Update connected lists in tandem; for instance, when an item is marked 'Completed' in one list, an entry in another related list is updated.
- Initiate workflows involving other applications such as notifying a Teams channel or updating a Planner task based on SharePoint list activities.

SETTING IT UP

1. While inside a SharePoint list or library, locate the "Power Automate" option in the toolbar.
2. Select "Create a flow" which opens a suite of contextual templates.

3. Choose a suitable template or design a custom flow as per the requirements.

ADVANCED AUTOMATION WITH POWER AUTOMATE

For users aiming to maximize automation capabilities, delving deeper into Power Automate allows linking SharePoint with numerous external applications and platforms, transforming it into a central automation hub.

POTENTIAL USES

- Seamlessly store email attachments in SharePoint from Outlook.
- Establish periodic reminders for tasks nearing their deadlines.
- Trigger CRM updates contingent on SharePoint list modifications.

SETTING IT UP

1. Open Power Automate and initiate the SharePoint connector.
2. Define specific triggers like the addition of a new SharePoint list item.

3. Configure desired actions, such as dispatching notifications on Microsoft Teams or other integrated platforms.

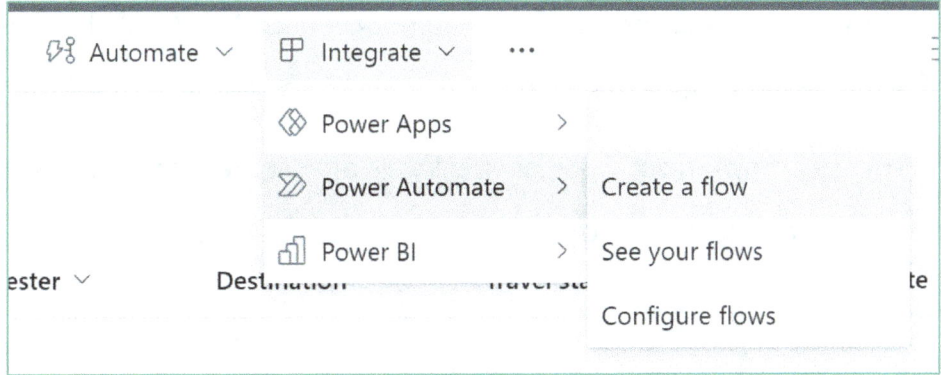

Figure 19 - Option to create a flow from a list or library ribbon menu

ELEVATING EFFICIENCY WITH BPA: A PRACTICAL EXAMPLE

Imagine a scenario where new project proposals need approval. Instead of manually checking for submissions and routing documents for review, SharePoint's business process automation can be your digital traffic director:

1. **Workflow initiation:** When a new project proposal is uploaded, SharePoint's workflow is triggered automatically.

2. **Assigning tasks:** The workflow assigns tasks (in Planner or Microsoft Lists) to respective approvers, sending notifications and due dates.

3. **Review and approval:** Approvers receive an alert, access the proposal, and provide their feedback—all within SharePoint.

4. **Seamless notifications**: Automated notifications keep stakeholders informed at each stage, reducing delays and uncertainty.

5. **Process completion:** Once all approvals are secured, the proposal moves forward, just like a green light at a busy intersection.

Business process automation optimizes your digital landscape like an urban planner streamlining city pathways. You're automating routine processes, ensuring consistency, and minimizing bottlenecks.

Q | QUICK LINKS AND NAVIGATION

As we venture into the letter **Q**, our spotlight falls on **Quick links and navigation** within SharePoint. Much like street signs in a bustling city, these features guide users effortlessly, ensuring they always find their way in the expansive digital landscape of SharePoint.

NAVIGATING WITH PURPOSE:
THE POWER OF QUICK LINKS AND CONSISTENT MENUS

The effectiveness of a platform often hinges on how easily users can navigate it. With SharePoint, this ease is achieved through:

- **Immediate access with the Quick links web part:** Acting as shortcuts, quick links (like those shown in *Figure 20*) provide direct routes to essential sites and resources, streamlining frequent tasks and user interactions.

Additional resources

Employees & Worksplaces	Get the latest on precautionary measures, and more	Leadership Updates	Read updates from our leaders about the impact
Global security	Get the latest on travel, and work from home procedures	News & resources	Security awareness checklist, and preparing for what's next
News from the WHO	Get updates from the World Health Organization	News from the CDC	Centers for Disease Control and Prevention

Figure 20 - Example of a Quick links web part in Microsoft's Crisis Management site template

- **Consistent navigation:** To foster user familiarity, it's crucial that the menus remain consistent throughout SharePoint. Whether exploring the HR department or diving into sales figures, users should always know where to find what they need. Consistency in navigation is akin to having similar street signs across various neighborhoods in a city.

- **Recognition and direction:** It's imperative for users to recognize their location, understand their available actions in that location, and identify potential destinations from any SharePoint page (where am I, what can I do here, where can I go from here?). A blend of visuals and menus plays a pivotal role in achieving this.

- **Emphasis on search:** The search functionality in SharePoint stands as a beacon, guiding users to their desired destination swiftly. When well-maintained and correctly set up, it becomes the most efficient tool to locate resources.

ELEVATING USER EXPERIENCE: WHY NAVIGATION MATTERS

SharePoint's Quick Links and Navigation do more than just direct users. They:

- **Promote user adoption:** Clear and intuitive navigation directly influences user adoption rates. When users can effortlessly find what they're looking for, they're more likely to engage and rely on the platform.
- **Offer tailored paths:** While consistency is key, SharePoint also allows for tailored navigation, reflecting the unique priorities of different teams or departments.
- **Prioritize key content:** Through Quick Links, highlight essential documents or sites, ensuring they stand out and are easily accessible.
- **Aesthetic appeal:** Beyond functionality, the design of navigation elements can enhance user engagement and overall satisfaction.

In the vast realm of SharePoint, navigation tools like Quick Links play the role of compass and map combined. They not only steer users in the right direction but ensure the journey is smooth and enjoyable.

R | RECYCLE BIN MANAGEMENT

RETRIEVING LOST TREASURES

In SharePoint's vast digital landscape, our letter **R**, the **Recycle Bin**, stands as the city's lost and found department. Just as city residents might misplace items only to later retrieve them, SharePoint offers a safeguard for deleted items, ensuring that mistakes aren't permanent.

UNDERSTANDING SHAREPOINT'S RECYCLE BIN: A TWO-TIERED APPROACH

Your recycle bin on each SharePoint site is actually two recycle bins:

- **First stage recycle bin:** This is the initial pit-stop for deleted items. Think of it as the neighborhood's lost and found. Users (members) can retrieve their accidentally deleted files and items from here, offering them an immediate chance at recovery.

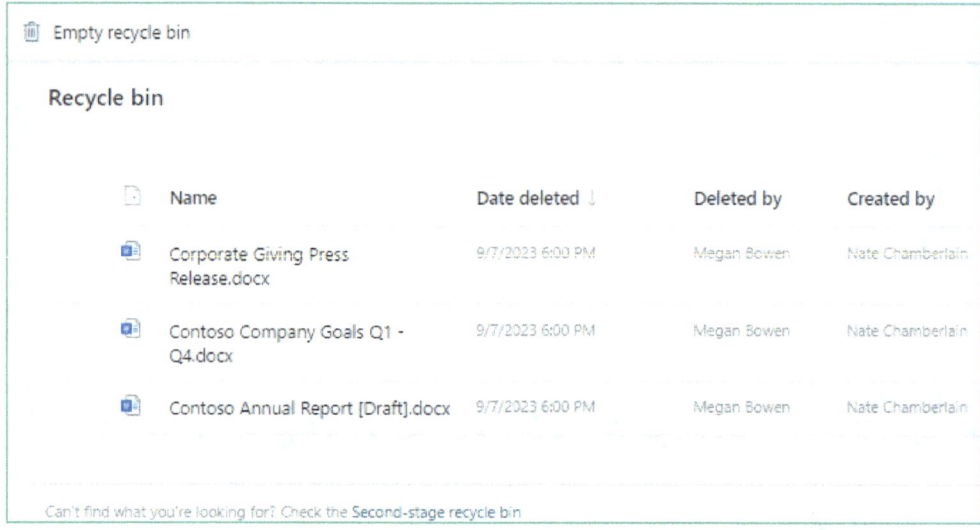

Figure 21 - First-stage recycle bin with a visible link to the second-stage recycle bin

- **Second stage recycle bin:** If an item is deleted from the First Stage, or someone empties the first recycle bin, it goes here, much like items from a local lost and found being moved to a city's central department. Site owners exclusively have the privilege to recover content from this stage, providing an extra layer of data protection.

Items deleted from lists and libraries are retained in both recycle bins (combined) for 93 days. For instance, if it has been in the first stage for 30 days before the first stage recycle bin is emptied, it'll spend the remaining 63 days in the second stage recycle bin before being permanently deleted.

EFFECTIVE RECYCLE BIN MANAGEMENT: BEST PRACTICES

So how do we best utilize our dual recycle bins? Part of it is regular review, and the other is informing our collaborators:

- **Regular monitoring:** Much like a city regularly cleans up its lost items, SharePoint administrators should periodically review the Recycle Bin, clearing out old items and ensuring valuable space isn't wasted.

- **Educating users:** Just as city dwellers are made aware of the lost and found locations, SharePoint users should be familiar with the Recycle Bin's functionalities, understanding how to restore or permanently delete items.

With Recycle Bin management, SharePoint ensures that unintentional deletions aren't catastrophic, giving users and administrators alike peace of mind in their daily operations.

S | SITE TYPES AND TEMPLATES

Navigating SharePoint is like traversing through a city, and every city is distinguished by its varied structures, each designed for a specific purpose. Similarly, SharePoint's sites and templates ensure that every project, team, or department has a space tailored to its needs.

EXPLORING SHAREPOINT SITE TYPES: THE RIGHT FIT FOR EVERY TASK

There are three site types to be aware of (four if you count child hubs separately from hub sites).

- **Team sites:** Think of these as the city's bustling community centers. Team sites promote collaboration, allowing members to share documents, tasks, and updates seamlessly.

- **Communication sites**: Resembling city bulletin boards, these sites are perfect for sharing news, reports, and updates with a broader audience, ensuring everyone stays informed.

- **Hub sites:** Imagine a city's central plaza, connecting various neighborhoods. Hub sites connect and organize related sites, providing unified navigation and branding.

HARNESSING TEMPLATES: STREAMLINED CREATION

From **Settings | Apply a site template**, a site owner can transform their existing site into a site ready to take on a specific scenario. There are several out-of-the-box templates to choose from as seen in *Figure 22*, but your organization can also deploy custom site templates tailored to your functions and initiatives.

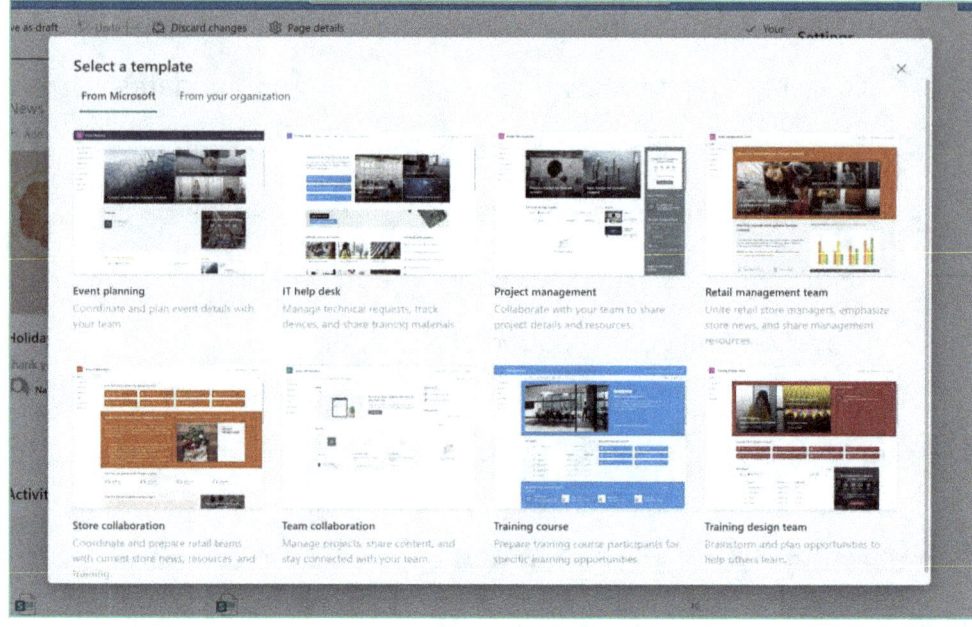

Figure 22 - Template options when applying a template to a SharePoint site

Here are a few examples of specific templates you might choose from:

- **Team collaboration:** This is the default team site template unless an owner has already changed it. It features news, quick links, documents, and site activity.

- **Store collaboration:** This template helps you communicate and share store news, assets, and training materials with staff. It features stylized quick links, a large news space, a people web part, countdown, and more.

- **Project management:** This template helps you manage and track your project details with your team, such as the project countdown, documents, site activity, project contacts, and more.

SharePoint's varied site types and templates empower users to build digital spaces with precision. By selecting the appropriate structure for their needs, organizations can ensure efficient collaboration, streamlined content management, and effective communication.

T

T | TASK MANAGEMENT WITH LISTS AND PLANNER

Managing tasks effectively is essential for completing our daily work, and SharePoint offers two powerful tools for team task management: Microsoft Lists and Planner. Let's explore letter **T, task management with Lists and Planner**.

These tools are like different transportation options in a city, each suited for different needs and preferences. SharePoint lets you choose the best tool for your situation and team for site integration, depending on the level of effort and skill required, and the degree of customization desired.

Getting started is as simple as creating the list or plan, then adding the underlying tasks with their relevant details:

1. **Create a task list:** Navigate to the desired SharePoint site. From the top bar, select **New** and choose **List**. Name it appropriately. Or if you're using Planner, navigate to Planner (*tasks.office.com*) and create a new plan.

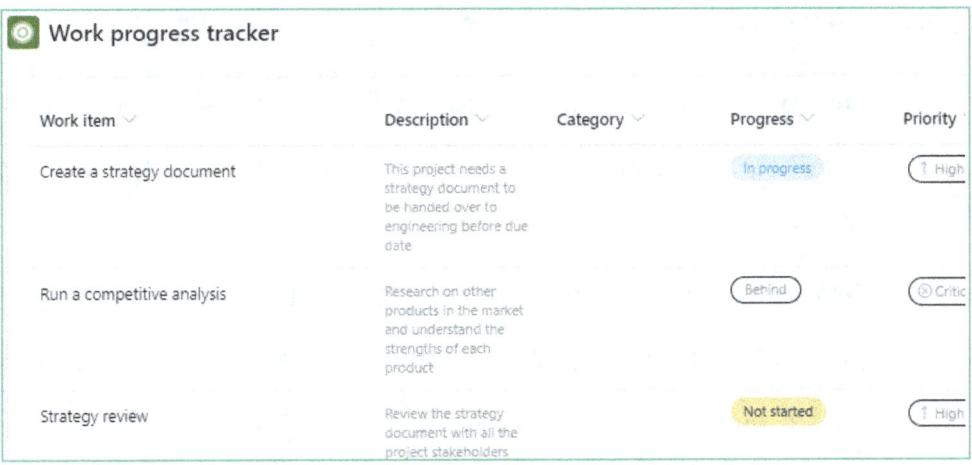

Figure 23 - The Work progress tracker list template in SharePoint

2. **Add tasks:** Once inside the list, click on **+ New** to start adding individual tasks. Or in a Planner plan, select **+ Add task**.

3. **Set priorities and deadlines:** Assign a priority level and due date for each task. This visualization helps prioritize essential tasks.

While the field names may differ depending on whether you chose to use a Planner plan, or a more customized list in SharePoint (Microsoft Lists), the concepts remain the same.

INTEGRATING WITH MICROSOFT PLANNER: A COLLABORATIVE APPROACH

Microsoft Planner, Microsoft 365's team task management tool, integrates seamlessly with SharePoint for a more collaborative task-tracking experience.

- **Linking SharePoint with Planner:** Simply create a plan and choose your existing team site's underlying Microsoft 365 group as its home.
- **Group tasks:** In Planner, tasks can be grouped by buckets (topics or categories), labels, progress, or assignment offering a clear overview.
- **Assign tasks:** Distribute responsibilities among team members, ensuring clear designation and accountability.

PROS AND CONS OF EACH APPROACH

Let's compare Lists and Planner approaches to task management.

SHAREPOINT LISTS:

PROS:

- **Inherent integration:** As a native feature of SharePoint, Lists ensure a seamless experience without needing external tools.
- **Customization:** Lists offer greater customization in terms of fields, views, and integration with other SharePoint features.
- **Granular permissions:** More intricate permission settings can be applied, ensuring task-related confidentiality.

CONS:

- **Limited collaboration features:** SharePoint Lists don't inherently have the collaboration-first approach that Planner offers, like task assignments or progress tracking.
- **Steeper learning curve:** For those new to SharePoint, Lists can be a bit more complex to set up and maintain.

MICROSOFT PLANNER:

PROS:

- **Visual layout:** Planner provides a card-based visual layout, making it easy to see task status at a glance.
- **Team collaboration:** It's built for team tasks with features like task assignments, comments, and progress bars.
- **Integration with Microsoft 365:** Tasks can be linked with Outlook calendar, To-Do, and more, providing a holistic task management ecosystem.

CONS:

- **Less customization:** Compared to SharePoint Lists, Planner has fewer customization options.
- **Separate platform:** Though it integrates well, Planner is still an external tool, which can mean managing another app for some teams.

Whether opting for SharePoint's lists or branching out with Microsoft Planner, the goal remains the same: to establish a streamlined task management process. Depending on team size, nature of projects, and collaboration needs, organizations can choose the method that aligns best with their workflow. Much like a thriving city with multiple transit options, SharePoint provides varied avenues for successful task management.

U

U | UNIFIED SEARCH EXPERIENCE

YOUR DIGITAL COMPASS

Diving into the vast expanse of SharePoint Online, the unified search experience emerges as your compass. In a realm brimming with data, content, and conversations, just as in bustling cities where signs guide the way, the search function ensures you reach your destination swiftly and efficiently.

MASTERING THE SEARCH: UNCOVERING DIGITAL TREASURES

As you venture into SharePoint Online, understanding the core tenets of the unified search experience ensures you always find your path:

- **Global search:** Positioned at the top, start by inputting your query. Like city street signs pointing directions along your drive, SharePoint Online offers real-time suggestions as you type offering shortcuts to your destination.

- **Advanced filtering:** After initiating your search, employ the filters to zone in on exact content, be it document types, verticals like sites or people, or more.
- **Content preview:** Just as peeking through a shop window offers a glimpse of what's inside, hovering over search results provides a concise preview, ensuring you know if it's the destination you seek before you select it.

STEERING YOUR SEARCH: BEST PRACTICES FOR A SEAMLESS JOURNEY

While SharePoint Online's search is intuitive, adopting certain practices ensures you traverse the digital scape with ease:

- **Metadata matters:** As descriptive signposts lead the way in cities, ensure documents and content are titled aptly and utilize metadata for better search accuracy.
- **Keep content current:** Regularly updating your content ensures relevancy and better indexing in search results.
- **Promote key results:** In SharePoint Online, your admins can highlight essential results or sites as Q&A, bookmark, location, or acronym result types, ensuring they're instantly recognizable and authoritative.

SharePoint Online's unified search isn't merely a feature—it's the compass at the core of Microsoft 365 guiding users through its expansive realm.

V

V | VIVA ENGAGE AND COMMUNITIES

SharePoint's Viva Engage web part and its underlying Communities feature serve as the connective tissue in a sprawling digital city, bridging spaces and ensuring that even in an online setting, personal connections remain paramount. This vital aspect of SharePoint creates an ecosystem where vibrant discussions, knowledge exchange, and expertise sharing are the norms.

PLUNGING INTO THE HEART OF COMMUNITIES

Looking to make your sites and pages more interactive? Look no further than the **Viva Engage** web part. In the expansive cityscape of SharePoint, embedded communities from the Viva Engage web part act as interactive public squares facilitation conversations by promoting community conversations, topics, and questions in a visible forum (SharePoint pages). Here, individuals from varied departments and expertise levels converge, creating a melting pot of ideas and experiences. They facilitate:

- **Discussion Boards:** Online forums where users can post questions, share insights, or seek guidance. These are particularly useful for newcomers eager to learn the ropes.
- **Expert Panels:** A space where seasoned SharePoint users offer advice, discuss best practices, and answer pressing queries.
- **Knowledge Repositories:** Centralized zones filled with user-generated content, whitepapers, guides, and more.

In the Viva Engage web part, you can configure settings like those shown in *Figure 24* including:

- Conversation source (Community, User, Topic, or Home feed)
- Specific source (which community)
- Filters (questions or all conversations)
- Publisher shown (on or off)
- Layout (feed or highlights)
- Quantity of conversations shown

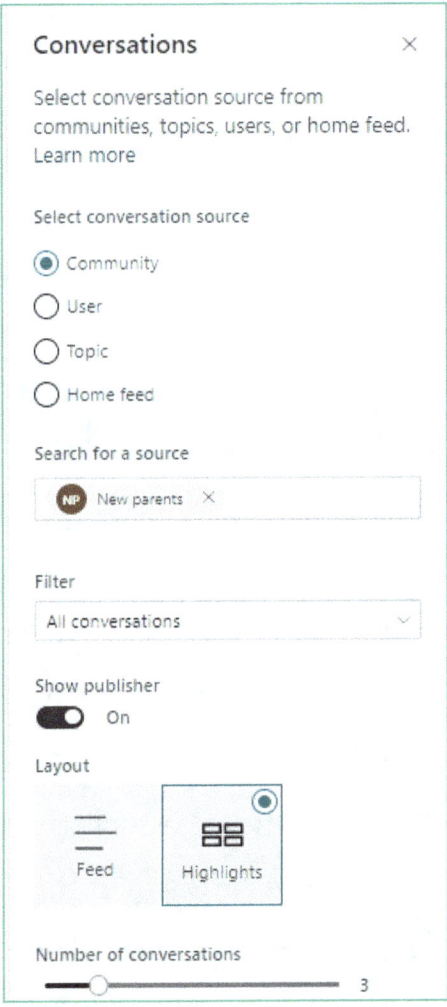

Figure 24 - Settings for the Viva Engage web part

Perhaps the next community you add to a SharePoint page will be motivated by one of these objectives:

- Cross-departmental brainstorming sessions
- Transparent feedback loops on ongoing projects
- Diverse viewpoints readily available for business decision-making

W | WEB PARTS

Just as monuments and sculptures accentuate the beauty and significance of a city, SharePoint's web parts serve to beautify and enhance its functionality. We've talked about several web parts throughout this book because they're essential components on every page or news post you'll ever see in SharePoint. These components can be easily added to pages, offering dynamic content, interactive elements, and personalized experiences to every visitor.

UNLEASHING THE MAGIC OF ENHANCED PAGES

In the realm of SharePoint, think of web parts as modular building blocks. Whether you want to display a video, add a news feed, integrate a map, or showcase a document library, there's likely a web part tailored for the purpose.

By leveraging the diverse range of web parts, you can:

- Add interactive charts and data visualizations.

- Integrate social media feeds or Viva Engage conversations.

- Display important announcements, upcoming events, or a quick poll.

- Enhance user navigation through breadcrumbs or quick links.

STEPS TO ADD A WEB PART TO YOUR SHAREPOINT PAGE

1. Navigate to the SharePoint page you wish to edit.

2. Select **Edit** at the top right corner.

3. Place the cursor where you'd like the web part to appear.

4. Select the + button that appears, opening a panel showcasing available web parts.

5. Browse or search for the desired web part, then select it to insert.

6. Customize the web part properties as needed, then hit **Publish** or **Republish** to make the changes live.

An essential aspect of SharePoint's utility lies in its capability to manage and showcase documents. With web parts, we can expand beyond storage to offer glimpses or interactivity in new ways such as:

- Highlight essential documents, making them readily accessible on a particular page without duplicating the actual documents.

- Showcase a specific view of files sorted by categories or departments.

- Fetch and display Microsoft 365 documents relevant to the logged-in user.

My personal favorite web part is the **Highlighted content** web part because it has immense flexibility compared to others. You can:

- Show all content or just content targeted towards a particular user or meeting specific criteria,
- Include as few or as many libraries across sites as you wish,
- Display results in a variety of ways,
- and more.

Figure 25 gives just a glimpse of some of the settings for this web part.

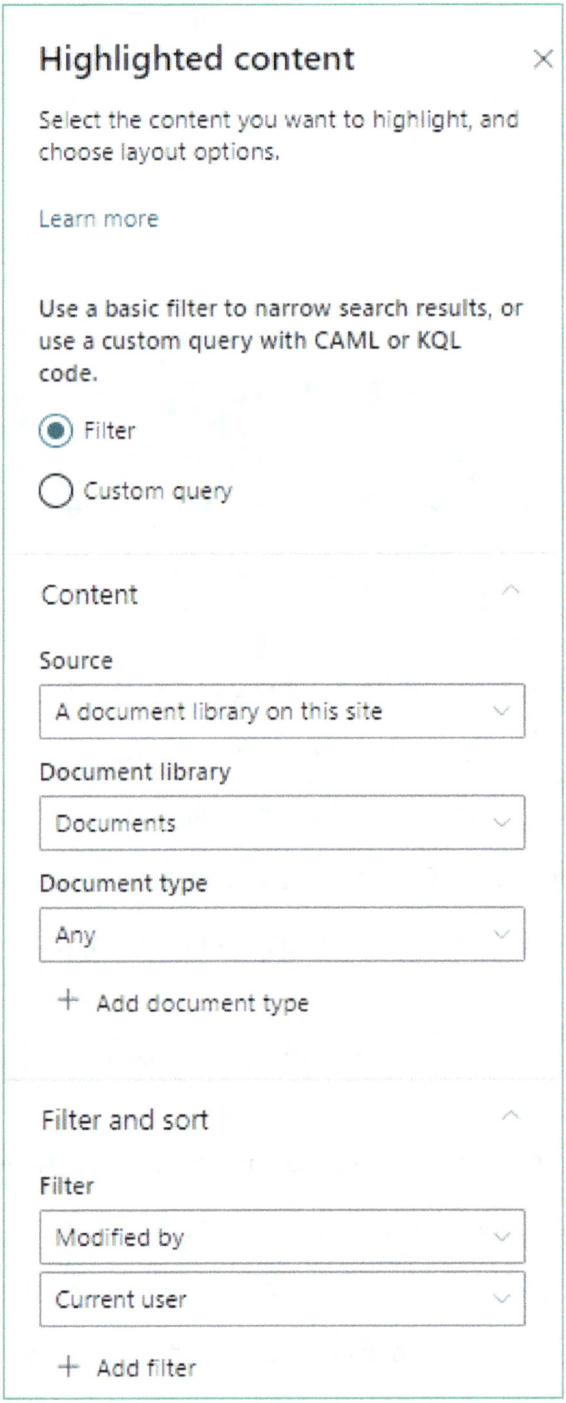

Figure 25 - SharePoint's Highlighted content web part settings panel

X | EXTENSIBILITY WITH SHAREPOINT FRAMEWORK (SPFX)

At the crossroads of SharePoint, where out-of-the-box functionality might seem limiting for some specific needs, the SharePoint Framework (SPFx) emerges as the signpost, pointing the way to extended possibilities. SPFx offers an avenue to tailor SharePoint's landscape more closely to your organization's unique needs.

CURIOUSITY MEETS CUSTOMIZATION: WHAT IS SPFX?

SPFx is SharePoint's modern framework for custom development. It provides a secure and efficient way to extend SharePoint's features. Even for the end-user or power user, understanding the potential of SPFx can help in conceptualizing solutions that may not have seemed possible within the confines of native SharePoint.

CUSTOM SOLUTIONS

- **Web parts:** The heart of SPFx. Create tailored web parts that perfectly fit the needs of your team or department, from dynamic data presentations to interactive functionalities.

- **Extensions:** Extend the SharePoint user experience – modify native menus, provide additional navigation links, or create custom footers.

MODERN DEVELOPMENT

- **Responsive design:** SPFx solutions are designed to be responsive, meaning they'll look and function seamlessly across devices, whether desktop, tablet, or mobile.

- **Integration-ready:** SPFx solutions can easily connect with Microsoft Graph or other APIs, making data retrieval from across the Microsoft 365 suite a breeze.

TREADING THE SPFX PATHWAY: WHERE TO BEGIN?

For the non-developer end users and power users, diving deep into SPFx development might seem daunting. But understanding its potential and knowing how to navigate the initial steps can at least lead to fruitful collaborations with developers. Here's a brief guide:

- **Identify the need:** Understand the specific requirement not met by SharePoint's out-of-the-box features. Is it a unique web part? A particular kind of data visualization? Or an entirely new navigation experience?

- **Collaborate:** Engage with your IT or development team. Outline the concept, emphasizing the benefits it could bring.
- **Explore:** If you're tech-savvy and curious, consider exploring the basic tutorials on SPFx provided by Microsoft. While you might not dive deep into coding, understanding the basics can enhance collaboration with developers since you'll go into the conversation knowing the essentials.
- **Iterate and feedback:** Once a custom solution is in place, continually provide feedback. SPFx solutions are flexible, meaning they can be adapted based on user responses.

In the expansive terrain of SharePoint Online, the SharePoint Framework represents the frontier of possibility. It's where the paths of imagination meet the groundwork of technical expertise, leading to solutions that can transform the SharePoint experience for everyone.

Y | YOUR LEARNING PORTAL WITH VIVA LEARNING

CONTINUOUS GROWTH AT YOUR FINGERTIPS

Typically, we think of Teams when we think of encountering Viva Learning, but let's see why letter **Y** is **Your learning portal with Viva Learning**. In the dynamic digital landscape of SharePoint, the pursuit of knowledge and skill development is paramount for personal and professional growth. SharePoint and Viva Learning can synergize to create a holistic learning ecosystem within your organization.

FORGING A POWERFUL CONNECTION: SHAREPOINT AND VIVA LEARNING

The integration of SharePoint in Viva Learning enables you to harness the full potential of continuous learning within your organization.

- **Curated content:** Just as a city's art gallery features carefully selected exhibits, Viva Learning offers curated content from various sources, including Microsoft Learn, LinkedIn Learning, and your organization's internal resources. SharePoint libraries you have with learning or training content can also be made a source that surfaces within Viva Learning.

- **Personalized learning:** Think of it as attending workshops tailored to your interests. This integration provides personalized recommendations and suggestions, helping you discover learning materials that align with your unique learning goals.

CONFIGURING SHAREPOINT AS A LEARNING CONTENT SOURCE

To configure SharePoint as a source for Viva Learning, you must be a Microsoft 365 global administrator or knowledge admin. If that's you, you'll find the ability on the Admin tab of Viva Learning in Teams. Simply add **SharePoint** as a provider in the **Provider** list, then follow the prompts to configure SharePoint as a content source.

With SharePoint configured as a learning content source, your organization can centralize its learning materials, creating a structured SharePoint list known as the **Learning App Content Repository**. This repository allows for the storage of links to cross-company SharePoint folders containing relevant learning content.

With SharePoint and Viva Learning working in harmony, your organization's learning journey becomes a seamless, comprehensive, and personalized experience, fostering continuous growth and professional development in the ever-evolving digital landscape.

Z | ZOOM OUT:
SHAREPOINT'S ROLE IN MICROSOFT 365

SHAREPOINT IS THE FOUNDATION

In today's interconnected digital realm, SharePoint emerges not just as a standalone tool but as the underpinning of an entire ecosystem. Understanding its pivotal role within the Microsoft 365 suite is essential to succeeding in Microsoft 365 usage and adoption.

In this segment, we'll delve into the intricate tapestry of Microsoft 365, spotlighting SharePoint's critical role and interdependencies.

TEAMS | SHAREPOINT AS THE COLLABORATIVE BACKBONE

Imagine Teams as a bustling town square where individuals converge to collaborate. SharePoint forms the architecture of this space, hosting the files, storing meeting recordings, and facilitating content-rich tab integrations while members and owners in Teams create buzz through chats, calls, and meetings. Any file you work on within Teams channels is seamlessly stored in SharePoint, while any file shared in chats goes to OneDrive.

ONEDRIVE | PERSONALIZED STORAGE

OneDrive acts as your personal apartment in the vast city of Microsoft 365. Dive deeper, and you'll discover it's essentially a tailored SharePoint document library, adjusted to your needs, storing your files privately just for you (unless you choose to share one or several with other individuals) and ensuring they're at your fingertips whenever required.

PLANNER & PROJECT FOR THE WEB | THE CITY'S TASK CENTERS

Just as a city requires planning offices, SharePoint provides the file cabinets for Planner and Project for the Web. Attachments related to tasks, milestones, and plans reside safely within SharePoint's confines, ensuring contextualized access.

VIVA ENGAGE | COMMUNITY CONVERSATIONS

In a sprawling digital metropolis, there need to be places for communities to converge. Viva Engage (formerly Yammer) stores its files and documents in SharePoint, ensuring seamless access for community interactions.

MICROSOFT FORMS & LISTS | INFORMATION STOREHOUSES

Every city requires hubs to collect and disseminate information. For Microsoft 365, SharePoint fills this role for Forms and Lists. Whether it's collecting survey responses or utilizing advanced list capabilities, SharePoint ensures data is stored, categorized, and ready for retrieval.

POWER BI & STREAM | THE DIGITAL BILLBOARDS

SharePoint acts as the billboard space for Power BI dashboards and Stream videos. It facilitates data source connectivity for Power BI and ensures videos on Stream are stored and shared efficiently across the digital landscape.

Navigating a city requires understanding its layout and structure. Similarly, by grasping SharePoint's integral role in Microsoft 365, you're better equipped to utilize each app effectively, understanding the threads that bind them together.

As you continue your journey through the digital landscape of Microsoft 365 beyond this book, remember SharePoint's omnipresent foundation. It's not just about documents and sites; it's the groundwork on which much of Microsoft 365 operates. Embrace it, and you'll navigate the cityscape with greater ease and efficiency.

SUMMARY

As we conclude our journey through the alphabet of SharePoint capabilities, let's take a moment to reflect on the valuable tools and functionalities you've uncovered to navigate, collaborate, and thrive within this virtual cityscape.

A | ACCESSIBILITY

Leverage SharePoint's accessibility features for inclusivity.

- Screen reader support
- High-contrast themes

B | BUSINESS INTELLIGENCE AND DASHBOARDS

Embed charts or Power BI reports in SharePoint.

- Power BI web part
- Chart web part

C | COMPLIANCE AND GOVERNANCE

Ensure data protection and adherence to guidelines.

- Data Security
- Retention Policies

D | DOCUMENT COLLABORATION

Facilitate teamwork on shared documents.

- Collaborative Editing
- Version History

E | EXPERIENCES

Access and interact with SharePoint in varied ways.

- Browser Access
- Mobile App
- Integration with Microsoft Teams
- Kiosk Access

F | FORMS INTEGRATION

Gather and organize user data with forms.

- Creating Forms
- Data Collection

G | GRANULAR PERMISSIONS

Manage content access with precision.

- Controlled Access
- External Sharing
- Secure Sharing
- Guest Access

H | HUB SITES

Organize and design SharePoint sites.

- Site Organization
- Branding and Themes

I | INTRANET PERSONALIZATION

Personalize intranet experiences.

- Personalized Content
- Followed Content

J | JUNCTIONS OF DISCOVERY WITH VIVA TOPICS

Navigate content using AI insights.

- Content Insights
- Topic Cards

K | KNOWLEDGE SHARING WITH VIVA CONNECTIONS

Stay informed with SharePoint's news features.

- Company News
- Mobile Experience

L | LISTS REINVENTED

Structure and relate data using lists.

- Structured Data
- Tracking and workflows

M | MICROSOFT TEAMS INTEGRATION

Enhance teamwork with Teams and SharePoint integration.

- Collaboration Hub
- Document Sharing

N | NEWS AND PAGES

Engage with the latest organization updates.

- Stay Informed
- Share Stories

O | ONEDRIVE INTEGRATION

Store and manage files with OneDrive in SharePoint.

- Personal Storage
- Version Control

P | PROCESS AUTOMATION

Automate tasks and processes in SharePoint.

- Automated Workflows
- Integration with Microsoft Power Automate

Q | QUICK LINKS AND NAVIGATION

Navigate SharePoint efficiently.

- Efficient Navigation
- Custom Navigation

R | RECYCLE BIN MANAGEMENT

Manage deleted items and recover content.

- Delete and Restore Items
- 93-day Retention Period

S | SITE TYPES AND TEMPLATES

Establish sites with purpose in SharePoint.

- Site Creation
- Templates

T | TASK MANAGEMENT WITH LISTS AND PLANNER

Organize tasks using Microsoft Lists and/or Planner.

- Create lists with views
- Create plans organized by buckets and labels

U | UNIFIED SEARCH EXPERIENCE

Search seamlessly across SharePoint.

- Find Everything
- Filters and Refinements

V | VIVA ENGAGE AND COMMUNITIES

Engage in SharePoint's Viva Engage communities via web parts.

- Communities
- Collaborative Discussions

W | WEB PARTS

Enhance SharePoint pages with web parts.

- Enhanced Pages
- Document Display

X | EXTENSIBILITY WITH SHAREPOINT FRAMEWORK

Develop and extend SharePoint functionalities.

- Custom Solutions
- Modern Development

Y | YOUR LEARNING PORTAL WITH VIVA LEARNING

Centralize learning resources in SharePoint.

- SharePoint's relationship to Viva Learning
- Configure SharePoint as a content source

Z | ZOOM OUT: SHAREPOINT'S ROLE IN MICROSOFT 365

SharePoint underpins many Microsoft 365 apps.

- Teams | SharePoint as the collaborative backbone
- OneDrive | Personalized storage
- Planner & Project for the Web | The city's task centers
- Viva Engage | Community conversations
- Microsoft Forms & Lists | Information storehouses
- Power BI & Stream | The digital billboards

THANK YOU

Thank you, dear readers, for joining me on this journey through The ABCs of SharePoint. From Accessibility to Zoom out: SharePoint's Role in Microsoft 365, you've explored concepts that empower efficient work, seamless collaboration, and confident navigation.

As you continue your exploration, remember that this book is just the beginning. SharePoint's capabilities are extensive and diverse, awaiting your innovative touch.

I've enjoyed guiding you through this experience and hope you've found inspiration and insight. As you forge ahead in your personal and professional ventures, I wish you continued growth, success, and boundless productivity.

Nate

www.ingramcontent.com/pod-product-compliance
Lightning Source LLC
Chambersburg PA
CBHW072216290526
45794CB00004B/1763